BACK WITH

BY

ELLEN DOUGLAS BELLAMY

JANET K. SEAPKER, EDITOR

BELLAMY MANSION MUSEUM OF HISTORY AND DESIGN ARTS

WILMINGTON, NC

2002

Manufactured in the United States of America

All rights reserved. No part of this book may be reproduced or transmitted in any form or by any means electronic or technical, including photocopying, recording, or by any information storage and retrieval system, without written permission from the publisher.

Back With The Tide
By Ellen Douglas Bellamy

ISBN 0-9673037-2-9

Copyright © 2002 of Perspective John H. Haley
Copyright © 2002 of Foreword Chris E. Fonvielle, Jr.

Bellamy Mansion Museum of History and Design Arts
503 Market Street
Wilmington, NC 28401
(910) 251-3700

The Bellamy Mansion Museum is a stewardship property of
Preservation North Carolina
220 Fayetteville Street Mall, Suite 300
Fayetteville Street
Raleigh NC 27601
(919) 832-3652

Front Cover Illustration: Ellen D. Bellamy at approximately eight years old

Back Cover Illustration: Ellen D. Bellamy in her late eighties

Table of Contents

Acknowledgements: Beverly E. Ayscue, Executive Director, Bellamy Mansion Museum of History and Design Arts ... *V*

Perspective: John H. Haley, Ph.D., Emeritus Associate Professor of History, University of North Carolina at Wilmington ... *VII*

Foreword: Chris E. Fonvielle, Jr., Ph.D., Department of History University of North Carolina at Wilmington ... *IX*

Illustration: The Bellamy Home Claude F. Howell ... 2

Preface: Ellen Douglas Bellamy ... 3

Memoirs of Ellen Douglas Bellamy ... 4

Genealogy ... 41

Floor Plans ... 42

Diagram of the Property ... 44
Narrative by Jonathan Noffke, Former Director of Bellamy Mansion Museum of History and Design Arts

Wilmington Map ... 46

Area Map ... 48

Index ... 50

Acknowledgements

ELLEN BELLAMY GAVE US A VALUABLE GIFT when she wrote her memoirs in the late 1930s. It is, in part, from her writing that we know so much about the Bellamy Mansion and the people who lived here. The reprinting of *Back with the Tide* is a long-held dream of many people and I thank the Bellamy descendents who allowed this publication to be produced.

As with so much that happens at the Bellamy Mansion, it was volunteers who gave their time to help with this project. My most sincere gratitude is extended to Janet Seapker who spearheaded this project, footnoted the original text and edited the new additions. Both Dr. John Haley and Dr. Chris Fonvielle graciously gave us insight into the period and into Wilmington's history to help us better understand the circumstances in which Ellen Bellamy lived. I thank them for helping us bring this memoir into 21st century relevance.

Thank you to Katie Caison, Carlos Nazario, Penny Newhouse and Edward F. Turberg each of whom performed the tedious task of proofreading text. Nan Farley assisted with yet another preservation project by indexing this book and we appreciate her help. I also thank and acknowledge the staff at the New Hanover County Public Library's Local History Collection, Beverly Tetterton and Joseph Sheppard, for their research assistance and Jonathan Noffke, former director of the Bellamy mansion, for allowing us to reprint an excerpt from an article he wrote about the Mansion's gardens. Gene Ayscue, of the Bellamy Mansion staff, was pivotal in bringing this project to fruition through his design and organizational assistance and, as always, I am most grateful to him.

BEVERLY E. AYSCUE
EXECUTIVE DIRECTOR
AUGUST 2002

A Perspective

WHEN SHE BEGAN WRITING "BACK WITH THE TIDE," on 26 April 1937 (which incidentally was the seventy-second anniversary of Joseph Johnston's surrender to William T. Sherman at Durham Station), Ellen Douglas Bellamy was eighty-five years old and her life had coincided with most of the significant events in the history of the United States during the late nineteenth and early twentieth centuries. Among these were the Civil War and Reconstruction, the advent of the New South, the Indian Wars, the Spanish American War, the Populist and Progressive eras, World War I, and the Great Depression. None of these events are as important to the development of the United States as the Civil War that destroyed slavery, notions of secession, and redefined the relationship of states to the national government. The war also weakened the economic power and social dominance of the prewar planter class.

THE AUTHOR FOCUSED HER MEMOIR ON THE CIVIL WAR because it had a deep personal meaning and she hoped her story would be of interest to future generations and expand their knowledge of the "troublous" times during "The War." We do not specifically know why she thought conveying her knowledge was important or who among future generations might be interested in what she had to say. She was of a family that had belonged to the antebellum planter elite. One can surmise that she was writing for the survivors and descendants of this group in the hope of reconnecting them to a mythic past. Not exclusively a story of inspiration for others, it indeed seems as if her narrative is a belated lament for the passing of a way of life in the antebellum South.

REFLECTING ON THE DAYS OF HER YOUTH, she provides a nostalgic and romantic description of a time when there was happiness, abundance, and a hierarchical social order that kept races and classes in their assigned places. From the cradle to the grave, slave labor provided the basis for much of the physical and material well-being of her family and its associates. "The War destroyed this "golden age"' and it appears that she could not or would not redefine herself in response to the social and political changes in its aftermath. Even though her narrative meanders, and at times lacks geographical and chronological coherence, her perspectives on "The War" and Reconstruction paralleled mainstream interpretations as reflected in the writings of Ulrich B. Phillips and William A. Dunning. There is continuity in her disposition and worldview. Not timid, she passionately expresses her convictions and her prejudices, and she makes no attempt to hide her biases. While she claims to report much of her experiences through the eyes of a child, we must not forget that her words are those of an adult who was writing not during the 1860s, but in the late 1930s with ample time to embellish, alter or suppress events. After having decades in which to reflect on her experiences, she continued to use disparaging terms in reference to Yankees, carpetbaggers, and Republicans. She uses racial stereotypes when describing African Americans, but makes distinctions among them. The good ones, the aunts, uncles and others who provided services for her family, are not classed among the "niggers" who tended to be Union Army soldiers or politically active Republicans.

READERS ARE CAUTIONED against what some historians call "presentism" which is the practice of judging the past by contemporary moral or ethical standards. But nigger was a bad word when the author was writing just as it is now. However, history cannot be completely sanitized and editing it out of a reprint of the text would only diminish the integrity of the document as a historical source. The author was not a professional historian or a writer, and a close reading will reveal that her narrative contains hearsay, racy gossip, and internal contradictions and inconsistencies. But it also embraces social, military, urban, family, and architectural history along with genealogy, and an autobiographical sketch of the author. No doubt readers will react to and interpret her story according to their own perspectives; however, they will not get an objective and accurate account of historical events by reading *Back With the Tide* and nothing else. The text is skewed and misleading and has a potential for propagating myths. Nevertheless, it is an important historical document, and as such, it must be viewed with skepticism and subjected to the same questions and critical tests as other historical evidence. Information in the text should be cross-referenced with and corroborated with information from scholarly and unbiased sources. In particular, we should want to know how the author knew the facts that she frequently claimed were indelibly etched in her mind and if they approximate reality. There is no precise correlation between memory and truth. Age often affects what and how well we remember events. Moreover, memories can be manipulated and we often remember things for a long time that simply are not true. Think of the fairy tales we learned as children.

STILL, *Back With the Tide* is valuable in other ways. While writing her story, Ellen Douglas Bellamy's life was figuratively and literally collapsing around her. She was infirm, feeble, lonely and confined to the upstairs area in her beloved spacious house that was in disrepair. Never married and without progeny, to some extent her memories were her most important legacy for posterity and a contribution to family lore. She never explains why she chose a meteorological metaphor for the title of her narrative. Maybe she thought that as the incoming tide often brings to shore bits and pieces of things lost or destroyed, her text would serve as a reminder that "The War" is still with us.

JOHN H. HALEY, PH.D.
Emeritus Associate Professor of History,
University of North Carolina at Wilmington

Foreword

THE CIVIL WAR AND RECONSTRUCTION IN THE LOWER CAPE FEAR, 1861-1877, haunted Ellen Douglas Bellamy. Although written more than sixty years after Reconstruction ended, her memories of that period, related in *Back With The Tide*, were consumed by the Union occupation of the region, and especially her hometown of Wilmington, North Carolina. She recalled those times with mixed emotions—trepidation and courage, anger and fondness, remorse and longing. As a young girl during the war, her opinions about what she saw and experienced, clearly were influenced by her parents and other adults around her. Even so, they reveal strong and enduring recollections of good times gone bad in the South because of the war and its aftermath. To her dying day, Ellen Bellamy believed that the Yankee army had destroyed an idyllic and a romantic life in the Lower Cape Fear, one that the Bellamy family had helped build and shape, and enjoyed. Seven decades, three subsequent American wars, and the nation soon to enter a second world war, did not alter her views of the devastation and humiliation her family and Wilmington had experienced at the hands of Union soldiers. Those troubling days prompted her, or provoked her, to record her memories for her descendants.

WILMINGTON WAS ELLEN DOUGLAS BELLAMY'S WORLD. She was born there, lived there, and died there. But the Wilmington "Miss Ellen" remembered with nostalgia was the one that existed before the Civil War. In antebellum days the "city by the sea" was North Carolina's most populated and cosmopolitan urban center and busiest seaport. An active maritime trade thrived as great quantities of naval stores, wood products, and rice were exported to Baltimore, New York, Charleston, and the West Indies. Hoping to benefit from the lucrative trade, Ellen's father, John D. Bellamy, gave up his medical practice to become a planter. He owned thousands of acres of land in both North and South Carolina, on which slaves boxed pine trees for turpentine and grew corn, rice, and peanuts. The wealth his land and slaves produced enabled Dr. Bellamy to become a respected and an influential gentleman in Wilmington, serving as a director of the Wilmington & Weldon Railroad and the Bank of the Cape Fear. It also allowed him to build and furnish for his family an enormous and a magnificent home, now known as the Bellamy Mansion. Ellen was born into and grew up in a world of affluence, privilege, and comfort. Attended to by the family's enslaved servants, her wants and desires rarely went unfulfilled.

THE CIVIL WAR DRAMATICALLY CHANGED WILMINGTON and the world the Bellamys had known. Confederate sea captain John Wilkinson observed in *The Narrative of a Blockade Runner* that "the staid old town of Wilmington was turned topsy turvy," as it became the Confederacy's main blockade running seaport. Lacking industrial facilities, the South had to purchase weapons and civilian goods from European suppliers, which were imported on board swift steam ships. In an attempt to halt Confederate waterborne trade, U.S. President Abraham Lincoln declared a naval blockade of the South's coastline and its principal seaports, including Wilmington. The Union effort to stop shipping at Wilmington proved to be ineffective, because of the difficulty of blockading the treacherous entrances to the Cape Fear River. Consequently, Confederate shippers preferred trading at Wilmington, where the success rate for eluding the Union naval dragnet was about 85%. More than 100 blockade running vessels operated in and out of the port for more than three years, smuggling vital supplies for the Confederacy and earning great fortunes for investors. But the profitable business also attracted to Wilmington an odd mixture of humanity: soldiers, sailors, and Marines to protect government interests; buyers, sellers, and speculators to make money; and crooks, con artists, and prostitutes to take advantage of those who had money.

WHILE THEY MOSTLY SUPPORTED THE CONFEDERACY, old Wilmington families were dismayed by the transformation of their town into a congested, bawdy, and dangerous place. The streets verily swarmed with strangers, foreigners, and criminals; inflated prices on blockade-run goods wracked the local economy; and crime became rampant. Conditions worsened when, in August 1862, the blockade runner Kate brought yellow fever to Wilmington. Soon the city was gripped by a terrible epidemic that claimed more than 600 lives before it ended with the onset of cool weather in late November. It was more than Wilmingtonians could bear. Those who could afford to escape the city did so, taking refuge in summer homes along the sounds, and in the piedmont and the mountains of North Carolina. Dr. Bellamy fled with his family to Floral College, a popular female institute in Robeson County that had closed its doors to students because of the war. The school's principal offered the college as a haven for wealthy patrons, advertising it as "proverbially healthy; and in these troublous times as safe a retreat as can anywhere be found." The Bellamys "refugeed" there for most of the war, although Dr. Bellamy occasionally returned to Wilmington to check on his home and business, and the state of affairs in the city. For little Ellen Bellamy the war seemed a thousand miles away from Floral College, as she recalled being happy there with family, relatives, and friends surrounding her. That is, until the Yankees came.

UNION FORCES CAPTURED WILMINGTON IN 1865 after a hard fought campaign that included the two largest naval bombardments of the war against Fort Fisher, the seaport's main defense located at the mouth of the Cape Fear River. After entering Wilmington on February 22, the Union army seized property for use as offices, quarters, and hospitals. General officers targeted grand homes owned by Confederate sympathizers, like Dr. John D. Bellamy, for their headquarters.

AS ONE OF THE FINEST HOMES IN WILMINGTON, the Bellamy house became headquarters for the post commandant, Brigadier General Joseph R. Hawley.

The Union high command appointed the North Carolina-born Hawley to enforce U.S. laws and supervise the occupation of the Lower Cape Fear. He turned out to be a tough and resolute administrator who ruled with an iron fist, as far as the Bellamys were concerned.

WITH THE WAR WINDING DOWN and Confederate defeat inevitable, Dr. Bellamy determined to take his family home to Wilmington. Even at Floral College, the Bellamys had been unable to escape the war, as Union soldiers of General William T. Sherman's army terrorized them on their northward march through North Carolina in early March 1865. Dr. Bellamy requested permission of Union military authorities to return to occupied-Wilmington, but General Hawley adamantly refused to allow it. He considered Bellamy a rabid secessionist who should suffer for his support of the Confederacy. "Having for four years been making his bed," the general declared, "he must lie on it for a while. I have no time to take him within the lines."

THE BELLAMYS WERE HEARTBROKEN. Eventually, Mrs. Bellamy was allowed to visit Wilmington, and was granted an interview with Mrs. Hawley, who had traveled from Connecticut to be with her husband. The meeting did not go well. Mrs. Bellamy was dismayed at having to receive consent to enter her own home, furious when she saw how the Yankees had abused the house, and disgusted by what she considered bad personal habits of Mrs. Hawley. She left without regaining possession of the property. In fact, not until September 1865, five months after the war, did the U.S. government pardon Dr. Bellamy for his allegiance to the Confederacy, and allow him to return with his family to the Bellamy house.

THE RUN-IN WITH UNION MILITARY AUTHORITIES had a profound effect on Dr. Bellamy and his family. They accused General Hawley and his staff officers of indecent, immoral, and lewd behavior during their occupation of the Bellamy house. To the Bellamys, their grand home reflected the prosperity, refinement, and grace of the South and its people. Its desecration by Yankees only reinforced their view of an inferior Northern culture. This notion deeply impressed Ellen Douglas Bellamy and is central to the writing of her memories in *Back With The Tide*.

CHRIS E. FONVIELLE, JR., PH.D
Department of History
University of North Carolina at Wilmington

"Back With
The Tide"

MEMOIRS
of
ELLEN DOUGLAS BELLAMY

Cover reproduction of the original 1940 printing of
Back With the Tide

THE BELLAMY HOME

Pen and ink drawing by Claude Howell
circa early 1930's

PREFACE.

I[1] am not attempting to write a story of the horrors of The War,[2] mingled with fiction and romance, like "Gone With the Wind," but just jotting down some actual facts of my own personal experience, and that of my family. I was not quite 9 years old when The War broke out, but those years are so vividly impressed on my memory I often go over them during the wakeful hours of the night, and I hope this may prove of interest to future generations who might otherwise know nothing of those troublous times. Indeed, this present generation knows too little of it. I will call my story: "Back With the Tide." The memories I have, are indelibly impressed on my mind, although I was a child at the time!

I am beginning to write this, today, April 26, 1937, at my home on Market Street,[3] Wilmington, North Carolina, in the eighty-fifth year of my life.

---

[1] Ellen Douglas Bellamy, May 11, 1852-January 30, 1946, fifth child of John Dillard Bellamy, M. D. and Eliza McIlhenny Harriss Bellamy.
[2] The American Civil War, 1861-1865.
[3] 503 Market Street, Wilmington, North Carolina.

MEMOIRS

OF

ELLEN DOUGLAS BELLAMY

Seventy-two years ago, on March 8, 1865, the Yankee Army numbering 20,000 strong, came to Floral College,[4] a little village of not more than fifteen houses, where we had been refugeeing off and on for several years. At the beginning of The War, my father, hearing of the depredations committed on the women and children of our Southland by the Union Army, deemed it unsafe to keep us so near Ft. Fisher[5] and the seacoast; thinking this little inland village would be a safe place, he and his friend, Mr. O. G. Parsley,[6] rented the college, which had been closed on account of The War. It consisted of two buildings connected by a covered way; Mr. Parsley moving his family there in 1861, the first year of The War, occupying the front house, and we taking the one in the rear, not moving up until September, 1862, when the yellow fever[7] broke out in Wilmington. Our furniture, however, had been crated and ready to be moved at any time. We had occupied our new home, 503 Market Street, Wilmington, only since February, 1861. Childlike, I did not dread the move as my elders did, but enjoyed the idea of the change—the thought of the freedom of the woods nearby, and the meeting of new acquaintances, was most enticing.

The Parsleys and our family lived most pleasantly together, my two older sisters[8] being devoted friends of the Parsley girls. In a little

---

[4] Community in Robeson County, North Carolina, about 95 miles west of Wilmington, named for a college for women which operated there from 1841-1878, except during the Civil War.
[5] Large earthen fort at the southern tip of New Hanover County, NC built between 1861 and 1865 to guard the entrance to the Cape Fear River and keep open the port of Wilmington for Confederate trade.
[6] Owner of Hilton Saw Mills, president of Wilmington & Manchester Rail Road and mayor of Wilmington.
[7] Yellow fever, a highly contagious, mosquito-borne disease periodically ravaged coastal communities. In 1862, Wilmington's population, black and white, was approximately 10,000. About half of the population fled the city to avoid the epidemic. Of the 1505 reported cases, 654 (43%) died of yellow fever.
[8] Mary Elizabeth (Belle) (1840-1900) and Eliza Bellamy (1846-1929).

while, Mr. Parsley bought a house in Lumberton[9], twenty miles off, and moved his family there. The Trustees of the college decided to reopen the school under the leadership of Reverend Daniel Johnson and family, so we moved to Steward's Hall on the campus, nearby, and our servants occupied a small building in between, called the Laboratory. There we remained 'till the end of The War, coming back home now and again. We were home when the first bombardment of Ft. Fisher took place. I can almost hear the sound now, as we sat in church,[10] on Sunday, December 25, 1864. My mother had planned a big dinner that day, and had invited many of her relations, and our pastor, the Rev. A. D. Hepburn; but, she had to recall the invitations, and we all went over to our Grovely Plantation,[11] ten miles across the river, where it would be easier to catch the train at Rowell's—a station of the Wilmington, Charlotte and Rutherford Railway, afterwards changed to the Carolina Central, and now the Seaboard Airline Railway. We remained at Grovely until the second bombardment, in February, when Ft. Fisher fell.[12] The Federal Troops captured Wilmington on February 21, 1865; they took possession of our home which we had temporarily vacated, and it remained General Hawley's[13] Headquarters a long time,[14] even after Lee's surrender. It was very galling, and my mother makes two reports of the "carryings on" in her lovely house, by the occupants. This was told by our neighbor who had remained in Wilmington, and had seen the brightly illuminated rooms, with wide-open shutters, and even into the bathroom, where, continuously, a nude man and woman would go in together! And, to show you manner of "men" "The Staff" (as Mrs. Hawley called them) was composed of, at the time my mother suggested moving in: One night, they gave a dance and invited their "lady" friends; during the hilarity of the evening, one of them gave birth to a baby in the high-post bedstead,

---

[9] County seat of Robeson County.
[10] First Presbyterian Church, NE corner of Third and Orange streets, in Wilmington.
[11] Described by her brother, John D. Bellamy, Jr. in his recollections, *Memoris of an Octogenarian,* as a plantation, being "in Brunswick County, . . . located on Town Creek and consists of nearly 10,000 acres."
[12] Union forces captured Fort Fisher on January 15, 1865.
[13] Wilmington fell to federal forces on February 22, 1865. The post-commandant was Joseph R. Hawley, a North Carolina native. He was a brigadier general in the U. S. Army.
[14] The Hawleys probably left the Bellamy's house in July 1865.

left in mother's room, where we had all been born. We gave that old bedstead to my brother Rob who was the last of us born in it. His grandson, Robert R. Bellamy, now sleeps in it, having requested it put in his room, so he could roll around without danger of falling out. I would love to see it since his mother has put draperies around it; but, being a shut-in, these days, of course that is impossible. My parents came down repeatedly to try to get possession of their home—to no avail.[15] They were stopped at the entrance by a guard, a "nigger" soldier! On my mother's first visit, while at my grandmother Harriss's home, corner of Second and Dock Streets, she came up to her own dear house, accompanied by a friendly neighbor, Mrs. Horace Burr, who was related to General Hawley, and had offered to introduce her. It was most humiliating, and trying, to be entertained by Mrs. Hawley, in her own parlor. Mrs. Hawley showed her raising by "hawking and spitting" in the fire, a most unlady-like act. During the call she offered Mother some figs (from Mother's own tree) which Aunt Sarah[16] had picked—our own old cook, who had been left here in charge of the premises.

It would take volumes to tell all that happened; I must merely skim over it. On their first trip here, my parents were stopped on the other side of the river by a burley Yankee soldier, who got in the buggy between them, and took them to an officer (provost-marshal, I think), for permission to enter the city. My father made several trips to headquarters in Washington City before they would grant him his "Pardon".[17] For what? For being a Southern Gentleman, A Rebel, and a large Slave Owner! The slaves he had inherited from his father, and which he considered a sacred trust. Being a physician, he guarded their health, kept a faithful overseer to look after them (his home being a regular drug store), and employed a Methodist minister, Rev. Mr. Turrentine, by the year, to look after their spiritual welfare.

---

[15] The Bellamys moved back in September or October 1865.
[16] Miss Bellamy often used the terms "aunt" and "uncle" to refer to the black slaves and servants who tended to the family. Such frequently were used by white Southerners as terms of endearment.
[17] Dr. Bellamy's pardon meant that he had sworn allegience to the United States government. It allowed him to reclaim his properties, including the Bellamy house; have his civil rights restored; and required that he relinquish his slaves.

Although The War was practically over seven months, we did not get possession of our home 'till September. Pa returned from Washington with the pardon, and the order for the restoration of his home.[18] He came directly here and was halted at the front door by a soldier. "All must halt!", he said, shouting his orders. In less than an hour it was completely vacated; in a little while my mother came with Tony, an old slave and handy man, and bade him open each room for her—but the bathroom could not be opened. She made him break the lock, and there, lying on an old filthy mattress on the floor, was a half-naked white woman that a member of the "staff" had left for his own use! (So we learned!) She jumped up when Mother accosted her, ran down the back steps, and disappeared. Tony threw the bedding over in the yard, and in a few minutes that went the way of the woman! Where? None ever knew! Then began the house cleaning by a number of servants, and plenty of dirt there was! Much damage had been done. For instance, the beautiful white marble mantel's in the two parlors were so caked with tobacco spit and garbs of chewed tobacco, they were cleaned with great difficulty; indeed, the white marble hearths are still stained, although every known remedy has been used! No furniture had been left in the parlors, except two mirrors which Mother had carefully covered with linen sheets. When the Yankees departed, the mirrors were left intact but the sheets were gone. They were, perhaps, the first linen sheets the Hawleys ever slept on. Furniture had been brought for their use from Mr. Donald MacRae's house,[19] a few blocks away; he was the father of Mr. Hugh MacRae and grandfather of Nelson MacRae, who married my niece, Marguerite Bellamy. On leaving here, the Yankees gave this furniture to a servant, who, being one of the MacRae maids, returned it to her owners. In our sitting room, our large mahogany bookcase was left as it was too bulky for them to carry off; but from its drawers numerous things were taken—among them an autograph album belonging to my brother Marsden. A number of years later, when my brother, John, was in Washington as a Member of Congress, this same Hawley, then a senator from Illinois,[20] told him of the album "coming into his

---

[18] Dr. Bellamy's pardon was signed by U. S. President Andrew Johnson on August 21, 1865.
[19] North side of Market Street between 7th and 8th streets, known as "the castle" because of its Gothic features.
[20] Joseph Roswell Hawley (1826-1905) was a Republican U.S. Senator from Connecticut, 1881-1905.

possession" when he occupied our house, and said he would restore it to him. However, he took care not to do it, although repeatedly reminded! Well, we all moved back home in October and my parents picked up the broken threads and began life again, as it were. Not an easy matter with the city under the rule of "Carpet-Baggers" and niggers! "Reconstruction Days!" They were terrible. No real recovery 'till the "'Riot'", in 1898, when our men banded with the Clergy, destroyed the printing press and office where the "Record", a negro paper, was published that had been sizzling with threats against our citizens, especially our women. Then they marched the Mayor Wright (Silas P.), an obnoxious Yankee, and all the city officials, including Postmaster G. Z. French, and a number of others of both colors affiliated with them, to the railroad station, made them board the train and ordered them never to return. They obeyed! Honorable Alfred M. Waddell was then elected mayor of our town and a reign of justice and peace began.

I will not go further, but return to our life at Floral College during the war and immediately after. I love that little village—life was so sweet and different there. We entered a select private school, just a short walk around—my brothers, John and George,[21] and I, taught by Mrs. Maria Nash, widow of Rev. Frederick Nash, a Presbyterian minister. I loved my teacher and feel that I learned a great deal during our few sessions there. My brother John and I had only gone to school here a short time before to Mrs. George W. Jewett, on corner of Third and Ann, and her husband taught the older boys in another room. My two older brothers had been taught by him before going to Chapel Hill,[22] where they were when the war broke out. They both soon left and enlisted in the army. Marsden[23] was in the Scotland Neck Cavalry, stationed at Wrightsville Sound, and Willie[24] was in Company 1, 18th North Carolina Regiment, which was soon ordered to Virginia. In their first battle his two chums and schoolmates—Wilmington boys—were both killed at his side. I remember going with my mother to their funeral at St. James Church—Willie Wooster and Duncan Moore;

---

[21] John D. Bellamy, Jr. (1854-1946) and George Harriss Bellamy (1856-1924).
[22] University of North Carolina at Chapel Hill.
[23] Marsden Bellamy (1843-1909).
[24] William James Harriss Bellamy, M. D. (September 18, 1844-November 18, 1911).

their bodies were brought here from the battlefield. My brother Willie survived all battles.

There were some very pleasant, congenial families living at Floral. Mrs. Eliza McLauchlin, a lovely widow, had moved there a few years before from Columbia, South Carolina, with four pretty daughters and six handsome sons; four of the boys were then in our army, and the youngest, Archie, enlisting the last year of the war at the age of sixteen; he lost a leg in his first battle. The girls were all at college there; the oldest, Janie, married John Kent Brown; Eliza, Willie French; May married W. H. Northrop (a cousin of mine), and Callie married Tucker French—all of Wilmington. Their mother finally moved down to live with them. There was, also, the Lilly family; Mr. Edmund Lilly keeping the only store with a little of everything. The stock became depleted and could not be replenished, so he soon sold out and closed up. I remember that my sister and Miss Lizzie Parsley purchased a box of white gloves—pall bearers—and died them in green tea and distributed them among their friends. Mrs. Lilly was a lovely woman with one daughter, Ella, about seven years old. Their family moved to Wilmington after the war, where Jennie, another daughter, was born; Katie and Berta later. Jennie died before she was grown and Ella married William Gilchrist, a native of Robeson County, but living in Wilmington. They were the parents of Lilly (Mrs. Hunter Wood), Eleanor (Mrs. Thomas Wright), Jennie (Mrs. Dudley Hill). Berta Lilly married Dr. Frank Russell, their daughter being Mrs. B. B. Reynolds. Another daughter, Jane, teaches in the mountains. The Swann and Davis families, from Wilmington, were also refugees, and our families were very congenial. The Betheas lived nearby and the McAllisters, Alfords and Cobles; Rev. Mr. Coble was the minister in charge of Center Church. I must not forget the Watsons; old Major Watson was a rare old character who kept the Inn, or Tavern; his wife and three old maid daughters made up his family. It was his house that General Francis Blair chose for his headquarters for the two days and nights the Yankee army was there. He was as a scamp, although later he was nominated for Vice-President of the United States; he was defeated. That was the only time my father ever "scratched" a Democratic ticket; he could not vote for a man who talked so insultingly to my mother and other ladies. (I'll relate that later—so much to tell). It was this same old Major Watson, the newsmonger of the village, that Josie

Davis and I with Misses Mary and Callie McLauchlin, taking a walk, approached for news, as it had been reported the Yankees were not far away, heading for us. Major Watson called out: "Run girls, the blue jackets are coming!" There they were, like a swarm of bees through the woods—and did we run! Josie got to her home, and the McLauchlins reached our steps with me! Like a pack of blood-hounds they rode up—such awful looking men! Long hair down to their shoulders, not cut since before the war. They were mostly from Indiana and Illinois. One of them really escorted the McLauchlins home safely, they having asked for protection. Then they rushed in demanding food and drink. We had only milk and a barrel of scuppernong wine, made the summer before at Grovely; when they tasted it and found it too new and sweet, they pulled out the bung and let every bit run on the ground.[25] My mother was made to taste all food before they would, for fear she had poisoned it. There was a jar of young vegetables, in brine for pickling; one Yankee tasted these, and not finding them to his liking, spit several times into the contents. They insisted that my father was hidden in a big wooden chest which contained the silk damask draperies and curtain from our double parlors in Wilmington at that time. He was actually on his turpentine farm[26] in Columbus County, which he later sold, and which is now the town of Chadbourn, North Carolina. In a twinkling of an eye, the whole house was ransacked; they appropriated anything they fancied, only missing a few valuables—jewelry, etc., hidden in a hollow space each side of drawers in the dark mahogany bureau; the drawers were revealed by removing the black marble top; this was broken in two pieces during transportation. A black silk dress pattern of twenty yards, at $100.00 per yard, (Confederate money, of which we had plenty), was rolled into a small package and hid in a new chamber with a top, way under the bed! Some flat silver and the new silver cake baskets were hidden among trash and rubbish under crated furniture in the lumber room;[27] another big square tin cake-box full of silver was buried on the lot, at side of the front steps near the root of a big tree; the ground was thickly covered with leaves; surprisingly, it escaped their bayonet thrusts, which were made every few feet, feeling for buried treasures.

---

[25] Scuppernong wine is a sweet wine made from a variety of muscadine grape which is cultivated in eastern North Carolina especially for wine production.
[26] The farm was located at Grist.
[27] Storage room.

The silver forks, used at every meal, my mother wore down her stocking legs for several days, the prongs of one inflicting a painful little wound on the calf of her leg! Dresses were worn long to the ground, those days! By the way, I have heard my mother tell that those forks were the second set ever in Wilmington; steel forks with bone handles to match knives were used altogether. Mr. T. W. Brown,[28] father-in law of Uncle Dr. W. W. Harriss, the jeweler here, showed mother a set he had just bought for his wife on a trip to New York. She was so enthused she got him to order a set for her. Such a curiosity! Her friends all came to see them; that was about 1845. They are still in use, the prongs much worn and sharp, but all the silver still intact.

To return to those terrible days. My mother and sister, Mary E., feeling the responsibility in Pa's absence, were very nervous and afraid—while I, too young to realize conditions, felt no fear of the Yankees but walked around singing our Southern songs and repulsing their saucy remarks. One day, Johnnie rushed in saying, "Oh, they've wrung Stonewall Jackson's head off and are chasing General Lee to kill him!" (Two favorite roosters in his flock!) My mother escorted by D. L. Russell, Jr.,[29] afterward a Republican judge, went to General Blair's headquarters to ask for a guard to protect us. (Even at that time, though we did not realize it, Mr. Russell was hand and glove with the Yankees). The general turned with an oath, and said: "I'll do nothing for you! Your husband is such a D—- Rebel!" About the same hour, Mrs. Peter W. McEachern, whose husband had been killed in battle in Virginia, who had lived six miles in the country with her two little girls and servants, moved in to Major Watson's for protection, bringing with her carriage horses and her husband's horse that had been sent home from Virginia. Suddenly she saw the Yankee soldiers astride her horses riding away. She rushed to General Blair and implored him to restore her husband's horse, at least. He said: "Kiss me and I will grant your request." She replied, "You rascal! I would die first!" So, she never saw her horses again. Do you wonder that my father refused to vote for him when he ran for Vice-President, with Seymour, on the Democratic ticket? Or that he was thankful

---

[28] Renowned Wilmington silversmith and jeweler who was in partnership with William Anderson in the mid-nineteenth century.
[29] Daniel Lindsay Russell, owner of Winnabow Plantation in Brunswick County, North Carolina.

when he was defeated? There we were, with no protection, until a surgeon—Dr. Boushea—rode up and asked for a room; when told all bedrooms were occupied by a Captain Sharp and other officers, he suggested spreading his rugs in our parlor and occupying that. He proved a "friend in need" and treated mother and sister with respect, but was a thief with it all; he showed us a pocket full of jewelry, and said he had "captured" those handsome rugs in Cheraw,[30] as they came through. But, he had guard kept continuously on our front porch until the army left, late next day; he even offered some food—(our own, prepared in our kitchen and spread for the officers) but the offer was not accepted. We were afraid; no one felt like eating. A year afterwards, sister and I recognized the same man sitting with a crowd in front of a Republican newspaper office on Market Street, between Second and Third. He had seen us before, down-trodden, in our homespun dresses, so at this second inspection we were delighted to have on our "Sunday best," and holding up our heads. The house we occupied then, Steward's Hall, had a long dining room in rear; one end we used as a kitchen, and the remainder of that long room was packed from floor to ceiling with corn, peanuts in bags, and other foods, many of them brought from our own commissary department, at Grovely Plantation, but marked C. S. A.[31] for protection! We had a small pantry where our daily provisions were kept. We had a large supply of meats stored in a smoke-house across the street belonging to a house rented by my father and occupied by a family of negroes from our Grovely Plantation. It seemed as if Providence had smiled on us. Such crops and increase in flocks and herds were never known before. The Yankees swore it was a Rebel Commissary Department, and in a few minutes every vestige was gone! Whole bags of corn emptied on the ground for one horse to eat! Of course, most of it was wasted, yet we wondered the men were not made sick eating so many raw peanuts. I told them I hoped it would make them desperately sick! Every piece of meat was gone, except one fowl which was hidden behind a post, and we found it many days afterwards. A barrel of sorghum went sour—so no more molasses peanut candy! Our servants—cooks, maids, nurse, and wash maids—were completely

---

[30] In Chesterfield County, South Carolina, just south of the North Carolina state line.
[31] Confederate States of America.

demoralized, and when the Yankees offered to bring them back to Wilmington, every one of them left us! You could hardly blame them, ignorant creatures, who did not like it up there and were anxious to get home. Guy, the coachman, came to Mother, and said he did not want to leave, but the Yankees made him, after taking his good shoes for themselves, and making him go bare-footed. They had also taken my brother John's new, homemade shoes, and left him barefooted on a cold, rainy, sleety day. Just before the army moved away my brother Robbie,[32] a four-year old baby, cried for food. I never knew 'till then how it felt to be hungry. The guard, an old Irishman, who had been drafted, said he did not believe in war; he went to his tent when about to start off and brought a tin cup of meal to Robbie. We had nothing to eat, no wood (they had burned up every fence, no fire)! After much effort, we got a pan of fire coal from a neighbor and made a little fire in our bedroom, cooked a pone of corn bread and gave some to each of our crowd. Early next day, Mr. D. L. Russell (Father of my brother's widow) who had bought a farm eight miles from where we were, heard about our plight, sent us two negro women and a load of provisions. But for his kindness, we would have been in a terrible predicament. Those servants came in handy, too, as ours were gone with the army, heading for Wilmington. Joan, our nurse, a very unattractive negro wench, who already had two children (never been married), rode down in the ambulance with Hickenlouper—an adjutant, I believe! Nine months from that night she gave birth to twins, both mulattos, who died while small children. Her eldest child, Caroline, a nice little girl, nine years old then, was Mother's little maid for a long time, following her from foot to foot. She is still living, though feeble, and for a number of years was nurse and trusted maid for Douglas and Placide Taylor. We took none of the servants back, except Mary Ann, and when she had a chance to go North, some years later, my father advised her to take advantage of it, thinking the climate in Pittsburgh, Pa., would be good for her weak lungs. She nursed Kenneth Burgwin (now a prominent lawyer) from babyhood until he was quite a big boy. She died a few years ago at a ripe old age.

Shortly after Mr. Russell's contribution to us, Mr. John A. Sanders, residing four miles away, and my aunt-in-law's father, sent a cart load

---

[32] Robert Rankin Bellamy (1861-1926).

of food—meat, meal, etc. The next day, Mr. Nicholas Nixon, when in Laurinburg,[33] sent us rye flour, etc. We really felt rich after having been reduced to want. My father had long been about the richest man around here and we had lived so luxuriously in spite of war. Had the war lasted we would have been underfed and of the outside world. At home, we had provisions of all kinds, raising cotton, spinning and weaving our cloth, both cotton and wool, for we had a large flock of sheep as well as a big herd of cattle and many hogs. There were deer a plenty in the surrounding woods, fish in the nearby creeks, and birds of many kinds besides our poultry—fowls, turkeys, ducks, geese, peafowls, etc. We tanned the leather and made our shoes. Richmond, one of our slaves, cut his knee and thus was disabled for doing accustomed work of cutting wood; so Pa apprenticed him for a time to a Mr. Hewett, a shoemaker in Wilmington, and Richmond became quite an expert. His shoes would bear inspection by the most fastidious. My sister would make the uppers of little shoes from old pants or scraps of heavy cloth for my baby brother, and Richmond would sole them. We were all quite proud of them. We were over at Grovely where all this was going on, on a little vacation, the spring and part of the summer of 1864. My brother Marsden came home from camp with typhoid fever and my sister Mary had it at the same time. They were ill for a long while. In his delirium, Marsden would see a fly crawling on the outside net of his bed and exclaim: "There is another Yankee", and aim to shoot him. They both recovered and during their convalescence Pa kept one of his servants busy fishing all the time—as fish seemed to be their best diet. One of our women, Mozella, was such an expert spinner that her yarns were too fine and even for our looms. Mother took me with her to Mrs. Drew's, a first rate weaver, five miles from us, and got her to weave a bolt of beautiful white flannel from Mozella's yarn. It was used then, and long afterwards, for skirts for all our family and kin. Guy, our coachman, drove us in the rockaway[34] with one of the iron-gray carriage horses. On our return trip, late in the afternoon, when we were three miles from home, the horse suddenly reared and pitched. There in the middle of the road an eight-foot alligator made a terrible snort and stood erect on his forefeet in front of the horse, only a short distance off. A deep ditch

---

[33] Earlier spelled Laurenburg then in Richmond County, North Carolina, now the seat of Scotland County.
[34] A light, low, four-wheel carriage with a fixed top and open sides.

was on each side of the road and prevented turning the vehicle; Guy finally succeeded in backing the horse enough for us to get out, cross the ditch and walk back to Grovely. The alligator was supposed to have come up from the creek through one of those ditches, and being awakened from his dormant state by the warm weather, was in search of prey—frogs or wild animals. We hated to leave Guy there in the "jaws of death," we thought, but he insisted upon staying with the horse. It was almost dark when we got home and reported. My brother Willie who was home on sick furlough took several negro men, mule back, with guns, etc. They found Guy and the alligator almost where we left him. They fired at the alligator but shot would not penetrate his thick tough hide, so they had to beat him to death with lightwood knots,[35] leaving him there 'till next evening (Tuesday); then they loaded him into a cart (the long tail dragging behind), drawn by Henry Clay, a gentle old horse, long since too old to work. They skinned him intending to tan the hide but the Yankees appropriated it like most everything they put their hands on. We came to town soon after, my brothers returning to their respective places. Marsden the year before had left the Cavalry Company and enlisted in Confederate States Navy, his ship, the "Richmond" stationed off the Virginia coast. We remained in town 'till the bombardment of Fort Fisher. On my father's last visit to Floral before the Union Army's raid, he took Andy McLauchlin and me with his tin box of valuable papers to an old smoke house across the road, back of a house he had rented and put two families of negroes from Grovely (they also left with the army—returning to Grovely) and buried the box, telling us to remember where it was in case anything happened to him. Excepting one jowl, the Yankees took all the meat hanging there (such a quantity of it). The box remained intact and several months afterwards we went with him again and dug it up. All communications were cut off between there and Wilmington; he could hear nothing from us. Lee had surrendered[36] and filled us all with grief. However, Pa started from Columbus County in an old buggy or rockaway with an old mule, corn and fodder piled up for feed not knowing whether he would ever reach us alive, having to pass through

---

[35] A heavy, pitch-filled knot from a pine tree.
[36] Robert E. Lee, commanding general of the Confederate army, surrendered to Union General U. S. Grant at Appomattox Courthouse, Virginia on April 9, 1865, effectively ending the Civil War.

such a dangerous region, "Scuffletown,"[37] the home of Henry Berry Lowery—a wild desperado, and his gang. They were blood thirsty and villanous, and had murdered a number of good citizens of that county (Robeson). He really encountered one of them carrying his gun who stopped him, looked over him and decided he would be no benefit to them, being so shabbily dressed and in such a delapidated equipage, let him pass on. He soon reached Lumberton, drove up to Mr. Parsley's and heard the first tidings from us; to his surprise found my sister Eliza stranded there, having been visiting the Parsleys for some time and unable to get to us. In that way she had escaped the Yankees raid on us, only about 100 of these straglers [*sic*.] having visited Lumberton. So Pa brought her to us—and there was a happy reunion. Just after leaving Lumberton they passed Morrisey's Mill Pond and saw hundreds of terrapins sunning themselves on the logs. He stopped and filled an empty feed bag with them and brought them squirming under their feet. It was really a God-send for we hadn't an overabundance of food. The servants we had then had no experience with terrapins nor had my sister and I, but we managed to get enough killed and cleaned for a big pot of soup which came in handy. Just in the middle of our preparations old Gen. Alexander McRae[38] rode up on his way home from the army and enjoyed it with us. Every few days some old friend would come by on his way home. Those were always joyful occasions. One day we children were in the nearby woods picking up trash left by the Yankees—among other things, the springs and wheels of an old buggy which my brother George rigged up with an old box and hitched to an old broken down mule that had been left by the Yankees in place of several good horses. We found it very handy for hauling wood, etc. The old mule by good attention soon picked up, but was confiscated soon after we brought him to Wilmington with us, being branded U. S. A.! While roaming around we spied three men coming through the bushes, scaring us right much, but imagine our joy and surprise when it proved to be my brother Willie, his man servant Sam Leary and Mr. Knox McQueen. Sam proved a good servant to us for years after. A few days after that Rob Rankin, a boy of 16 walked up—he was with his father, Capt. R. G. Rankin, when he was killed. Capt. Rankin was a favorite cousin of Mother's. My brother Rob was named for him!

---

[37] A town in west-central Robeson County now known as Pembroke.
[38] Now spelled MacRae.

Of course, Mother took him in and proved a mother to him, his own mother (cousin Susan) having died with yellow fever in 1862. That was the last battle of Bentonville near Raleigh—Cousin John D. Taylor (Colonel) lost an arm in the same battle. His family were refugeeing in Marion, S. C., and old Col. Durant sent Col. Taylor's mother, wife and baby in his carriage to meet him. They got as far as Mr. Russell's who had sent his carriage over for us, to spend the day with them, so we took Rob Rankin who could tell them all about him. They had only heard he was alive but didn't know until then of the loss of his arm. Someone picked him up and brought him there so there was another happy reunion. I remember Walker as a baby then, 6 months old, dressed in a long pink calico dress—fortunate to have that, cloth was so scarce! When we got home from the Russell's late that night, bringing the Taylors' all with us (they returned to Marion next day), we found Pa and Eliza waiting for us on the front piazza. We had locked up the house and taken the servants with us. Pa learned from the neighbors where we were so he was content to wait. Well, after that, things settled down; we lived a free and easy life waiting and hoping to get back home in Wilmington. Pa spent most of his time between the two plantations, to get things adjusted but coming to Floral now and then and bringing mother down to intercede for the restoration of our home. I have already told of those trips and how long it was before we ever got possession of it. She would stay with grandma who happened to be here at her home, corner of Second and Dock. They had been refugeeing in Lumberton but came home on a visit just before Wilmington fell. My father was too old to go in actual service but drilled with the home guard every afternoon at the old court house square at beginning of war. His health was not good and he had given up the practice of medicine some years before. He had practiced very successfully a number of years here, having taken over my grandfather's practice, Dr. W. J. Harriss, at his death. He had studied medicine under him about 1837 and afterwards graduated at Jefferson Medical College in Philadelphia. While a student here in Wilmington he met and married my mother, Eliza M., eldest daughter of Dr. Harriss. He intended going to Philadelphia to practice but Grandpa died suddenly, not quite one month after their marriage, just as they were planning a honeymoon trip abroad. It was the custom in those days to wait a month. They had invited Cousin Laura Rankin (Rothwell afterwards) to accompany them as mother was not 18 years old and needed a companion. Of course, their plans were altered by Grandpa's death, the trip given up, and they decided to remain here with grandma, a young widow with 8 children younger than mother. Pa bought out the practice and office effects and carried on. They remained with grandma until birth of their third child, then bought and moved into the house just across the street where all the rest of our ten were born except Robbie; he was born in this house,[39] July 21, 1861, the day of the Battle of Manassas. All the ten lived to maturity except the eighth, little Kate Taylor, who only lived three weeks.[40] Now only my brother John and I are left, he 83 and I am 85. I am all alone in this big house with a companion, Miss Lina Stallings, who has been with me for 6 years—nearly all of that time I have been "shut in" and now am very feeble and not able to get downstairs at all. But I have a young couple, Dr. and Mrs. Junius Smith, occupying an apartment just across the hall up here. It is a pleasure to have them as a protection—they are kind and considerate of me and very congenial. I feel I have put off too long writing this. I am feeble and hardly able to collect my thoughts—my sight so poor too and I write with difficulty, but God is so good to me enabling me to keep my mind perfectly clear and my memory good, and while I'm very lonely here I dare not murmur. I have so many comforts and blessings and while never ceasing to miss my dear ones gone before, my loved ones and friends left are most kind and considerate of me, especially my brother John and family who live just one block from me, corner 6th and Market Streets. It is such a pleasure to have him during the summer to take his mid-day meal while his family are summering on Wrightsville Beach only a short distance away in these days of fast travel. My neice [*sic.*], Elise Verner, from Columbia, always pays me a visit during the summer. She is the only one now whose visits I always look forward to and enjoy, since the other dear niece, Ellen Taylor, suddenly passed away just one year ago—They were the daughters[41] of my very dear sister, Mary E. ("Belle") who married Mr. W. J. Duffie of Columbia, S.C. She died 37 years ago, and I have always felt toward them as my very own children. After my parents' death, my sister Eliza and I lived here alone in the old home, very congenially and happily, but God took her

---

[39] The Bellamy's house, 503 Market Street, Wilmington, North Carolina.
[40] Kate Taylor Bellamy (June 19, 1858-July 14, 1858).
[41] Born Eliza Bellamy Duffie and Ellen Douglas Duffie, daughters of Belle Bellamy and William Jefferson Duffie.

suddenly away, eight years ago leaving me all alone. My brothers, Marsden, William, George H., and Robert R., preceeding her not many years apart. My brother Chesley C., having died in 1881, only lacking a few weeks of being 21 years old.[42] He and Rob were both students at Davidson College and expecting to graduate the next year. Rob did return and graduate and afterwards studied pharmacy and was a successful druggist the rest of his life. Hargrove, his only child, is now carrying on his wholesale drug business. Rob's wife, Lily Hargrove, (sister of Emma, my brother John's wife) died just three years ago. They had a beautiful home next door to here.

To return to my story of the War; it would be incomplete if I did not tell of a typical Refugee Funeral in our midst then. The Davis and Swann families were only a stone's throw from us at Floral College and we were together almost daily. Josie Davis, the eldest daughter, was about my age and we were almost inseparable. She afterwards married a son of Bishop Gregg and moved away from here. The above families were lovely people, strict Episcopalians. Mrs. Swann, the grandmother, was a sister of Bishop Green. They were in rather straightened circumstances owing to the war and occupied an old store house, the only available one then in the village—the lower floor one long room serving as parlor, dining-room and kitchen, being divided up with the respective furniture. They would attend services at the Center Presbyterian Church in the grove nearby—but after returning from our service would gather their family together with any visitors (I was usually there) and read the Episcopal service. That is how I became familiar with it, never having attended an Episcopal church over three times in my entire life. A short time after Blair's visit there, Lizzie, her little girl, nine years old, was stricken with typhoid fever from which attack she never rallied. Every night for several months, my sisters, the McLauchlin girls, and other friends would sit up and help nurse her. Every garment of her clothing had been used up and no way of replenishing—so when she died my mother took a pretty little new nightgown of mine which Miss Jane Buchanan laundered beautifully, crushing the little ruffles around neck and front and put it on her—bound round the waist by a new white cord and tassell.

---

[42] Chesley Calhoun Bellamy lacked a month and a few days of being 22 when he died (September 29, 1859-August 7, 1881).

I remember how sweet she looked and how glad I was for her to have it. Then impossible to procure a casket for her, a negro servant ripped boards from their old stable and made a coffin which mother and Miss Jane lined and covered with a sheet and after a service at the house by Mr. Coble, Presbyterian Pastor, she was borne by my brother Willie and Platt Cowan (who was visiting at our house)—to her grave in a plot round the church. To add to the sadness, the grave had been dug too small and tho night was coming on we had to wait until, by the light of lightwood torches, the grave was dug long enough. Child as I was, can I ever forget it?! That same summer before we came back home my mother and father were in Wilmington a great part of the time and my sister had all responsibility of us younger children, but I enjoyed it thoroughly. She was so conscientous [sic.] she would never leave us and when invited to a picnic or trip anywhere would pile us all in the wagon and take up along. One I especially remember was at "Red Springs",[43] now the site of Flora McDonald College, then only a delapidated [sic.] little shed with steps for seats over the "Springs" and an old barn that they used for dancing to the music of an old fiddler. I was an odd child and enjoyed grown folks much more than I did children and was always delighted to go. I remember another occasion I long doted on—That was before the Yankee Army came. There was to be an exhibition at Mrs. Gages' school at Laurinburg, ten miles off, on the Railroad. My mother was at home up there and she carried her big carriage full of young folks including my sisters and their friends; among them, Lieut. Luther McKinnon, a special friend of my sister. He begged for me to go with them saying he would take the best care in the world of me. I went with them to Shoe Heel depot where they took the train. Mother yielded and I had the time of my young life. They danced way into the night and I sat on the steps to the stage with my head on one of the ladies' laps and slept most of the time 'till the train returned to Shoe Heel very early in the morning. The name of that Depot was so called on account of the creek running around the shape of a shoe heel. There was nothing there then except the station warehouse and the old turpentine distillery. It is now the flourishing town of Maxton. Lieut. McKinnon I referred to was a brave soldier at home on furlough—his home only a few miles from there. After the war he studied at Theological Seminary and became a consecrated

---

[43] A town in northern Robeson County, known earlier as Dora.

successful Presbyterian minister. Some years after he became Pastor of First Presbyterian Church, Columbia, S.C., where my sister was a member and attended, her husband being an elder and treasurer of Seminary for years. It was pleasant to renew their acquaintance in Columbia and their families saw a good deal of each other. That was about 1883—He had married Miss Addie Lee of Clinton, N.C., and in after years when his health failed he retired and went to her old home to live. Being paralyzed he would sometimes sit in his rolling chair on her front piazza and hold a service with a crowd of friends sitting on sidewalk. He died a short time after. She too is dead and I don't know what has become of their two children, Howard and Sallie Lee. On our last summer there, I was just that age to enjoy everything, especially the free life of country around. I had two girl friends, Ellen and Pat McKoy living about two miles away. How I did enjoy the walks out there, often spending the day. I attended Center Church and saw them every Sunday, often relishing a picnic in the grove around the church. It was the custom those days to hold two services and during the recess everybody ate their dinner which they had brought. And at intervals during the year they would hold a "sacramental" meeting enduring 3 days—great occasion—families visiting with each other and cooking cakes, pies and other good things for a week before. And the people were more "thirsty" for religion and never seemed to tire but enjoyed two long services each day—my! those were good old times and when I had to leave there, even to come home, it most broke my heart. I have never been back but once, visiting about six miles from there with Tom Russell and his wife Fanny, nee' Havens. They took me over to church; we rode all about the place and found everything changed and gone to rack and ruin. They are buried in that church yard, parents of Lindsay, Frank (deceased), Mary Bonner (Mrs. Moss, of Washington, N.C.), and Bryan Russell living way off somewhere in Texas. After our return home to Wilmington, though we were shocked by the terrible experience of War, life went on and things became somewhat normal. I picked up my studies as a "Parlor" scholar at Cousin Laura Rothwell's school, she having secured an assistant, Mr. Steinberg, who taught Latin, French; his career was short. I was glad, I had determined not to recite another lesson to him. He was too "fresh" to suit me, a German too. And the boys were sent to their respective schools except the two baby brothers. My eldest sister had graduated at Barhamville, a young ladies' college a few miles from

Columbia, S.C.[44] It was recommended by Dr. Robert Harllee of Mars Bluff, S.C., an old friend of my father's who had two daughters there. The girls became firm friends visiting each other several times. It was through them that my brother Marsden met their youngest sister, Hattie, and they were married soon after the War. She attended Barhamville, also. Sherman burned the college when he set fire to so many lovely buildings in Columbia. Sister painted all those pictures hanging in our parlors downstairs. A strange coincidence—Mr. Duffie, whom sister afterwards married, having a great mania for buying up land, had purchased the ground site of the old college before he met her; after his death they sold it. A few years ago a reunion of the old students or their descendants was held in a little lodge built on the grounds. My two nieces and a daughter of one, Mary Bellamy Verner, attended by invitation. I happened to be over there on a visit and was able to tell them the meaning and could recognize old photos, etc., found in a trunk of their mother's, all familiar to me but not to them. There were among them old reports and most complimentary letters from Dr. Marks, the Principal, to my father about my sister. The lot on which this house was built, 503 Market St., was owned by Mr. McCumber from whom father bought it in 1858.[45] He also owned the lot just east of us, bought by my brother Rob, later; his house was built there in 1896. This location was considered about the boundary—just a few houses beyond it.[46] The Gallows Hill was where the Old Ladies' Home now is, corner 9th and Princess.[47] My mother as a child, was sent with her nurse and saw a negro woman hanged there; when the sheriff [was] asked what crime she had committed, replied: "Nothing but killing old Mrs. Bradley" (her mistress).

---

[44] South Carolina Female Collegiate Institute in Barhamville, just north of the city of Columbia, was opened in 1829 to offer women a higher education.
[45] Brothers Robert S. and James N. McCumber sold the lot, just over a half-acre, to Bellamy by deed recorded July 28, 1859 for $4500 (New Hanover County Deed Book, QQ, p. 77). There was a new wooden house on the lot in 1849 when it was insured for $500. In 1853 it again was insured, then for $800 (New Hanover County Deed Books, FF, p. 420 and KK, p. 392).
[46] The city extended its boundaries in 1848 from 5th Street to 13th Street.
[47] Gallows Hill also has been cited to be on Market between 8th and 9th streets. "The Old Ladies' Home" was the Catherine Kennedy Home founded in 1879.

But as the town began to build up the gallows was moved to waydown South Front Street, "Dry Pond."[48] I remember as a little child going with my nurse and standing on the portico of the old Presbyterian Church on Front Street between Dock and Orange, and seeing two negro men "Scott and Peter" pass on their way to the gallow. They were condemned for murder! On a cart, sitting on their coffins, white suits on, long black caps on to be pulled down over their faces at the gallow! I'll never forget the sight! That church was burned to the ground in 1859; nothing was saved except the communion service and three big highback chairs to match table, a few hymn books. I recall how distressed my mother, sisters, grandmother and other friends were. I stood with them on grandma's upstairs back piazza and watched it burn and heard the bell toll once and then crash to the ground. In a short time our congregation bought a lot on Third and Orange Streets, a more desirable location and built the new church there. It was completed in 1861[49] and dedicated that same spring, the Rev. Charles Philips of Chapel Hill preaching the sermon. His wife was our old friend and schoolmate of Mother's and she entertained them at supper in our beautiful new dinning room. They, by the way, were the parents of Mrs. Mary Philips Verner, still living and the mother-in-law of my niece, Elize Duffie Verner and she is now on a visit to her in Columbia. When funds were raised for a new church, my Uncle George Harriss offered to give the bell, and two old bachlors, Mr. Eli Murray and Mr. Wm. McRary pledged themselves for the new organ, but before time for it to be installed Mr. McRary backed out, having just married Miss Patty Wiggins, from Enfield, who was an Episcopalian, and she wished his charity to go in that direction, if at all. They bought and lived in old Dr. Wright's home, opposite corner from St. James' Church, on Third and Market.[50] He died first and at her death having no children, she left her home and estate to her maiden sister, Miss Rowe Wiggins. Now the Colonial Dames are negotiating for it from her heirs and hope soon to own it and use it as their Headquarters House[51]. Lord Cornwallis made his

---

[48] An area south of Castle Street near 5th.
[49] Dedicated April 28, 1861; Gothic Revival structure designed by Samuel Sloan of Philadelphia.
[50] Burgwin-Wright House, SW corner of Market and 3rd streets.
[51] The house was acquired in 1937 by the Colonial Dames.

headquarters there for several weeks during the Revolutionary War.[52] My neice, Eliza Bellamy Williamson, is President of the North Carolina Chapter of Colonial Dames. Since 1912, they have held their meetings in our home, renting our former dining room and pantry (or breakfast room) on our first floor or English basement. They have been pleasant tenants and I will hate to give them up, if they move during my lifetime.

To return to our dear old Church; I am the oldest native member now and I love it as the "apple of my eye." The second building was destroyed by fire not many years ago, Dec. 31, 1925. Nothing saved, all gone—the beautiful memorial windows and everything. The present new church was completed about two years after—many memorials placed in it.[53] The Kenan family, Jessie Kenan Wise, William R. Kenan and Mary Lillie Kenan[54] giving the steeple and memorial chapel adjoining, in memory of their parents. Mr. W. R. Kenan[55] was for a long time one of our beloved elders. Mr. James Sprunt, also an elder, gave the organ in memory of his wife. There were more smaller memorials too numerous to mention. Dr. A. D. P. Gilmour is now our beloved pastor, and has entered his fifteenth year, in Wilmington. I could write volumes on this subject but I must remember "This is a story of the War." I digress from writing of this old home of mine which although sadly in need of repairs outside is so well built and of such good material, the interior in such splendid condition, no leaks or fallen plastering as in most old houses, but too big for a poor old weak, feeble woman to look after. The garden, once the most beautiful in Wilmington, is now a "thing of the past"—only old evergreens and magnolias left; but I love it and try at least to have it kept clean. The war coming so soon after the house was built, the fence or iron railing was not put up 'till several years after;[56] it was bought with money

---

[52] Some historians question Cornwallis using the Burgwin-Wright House as his headquarters.
[53] The new church, First Presbyterian, was dedicated November 18, 1928.
[54] Miss Bellamy is referring to William Rand Kenan, Jr.; Mary Lillie Kenan Flagler Bingham died in 1917; the other donor was another daughter, Sarah Graham Kenan.
[55] W. R. Kenan was Captain William Rand Kenan. The chapel was given in memory of him and his wife, Mary Hargrave Kenan.
[56] The fence was erected after Market and 5th streets were widened, sometime between 1866 and 1873. In 1873, photographer Rufus Morgan took many of his stereographs including one of the Bellamy family in front of their home; it shows the fence (see inside cover).

realized from sale of rosin and turpentine. Then the garden was laid out. After getting clear of nut grass, beautiful oak trees were planted soon after we moved here, in front of house; when grown to considerable size, they were cut down by the town authorities. Confederate Robt. Ransom, Chief of Police at the time (who had moved here and he and his wife opened a girls' boarding school in the Costin house, corner of Dock and Fifth Streets, now occupied and owned by Dr. Farthing)—decided to widen the street, and although workmen were starting the walk for our iron railing, stopped the work and required Pa to throw about ten feet of our front lot into the street—thereby putting the trees too far out; thus in a little while all our beautiful trees were cut down. My father took it terribly to heart but had to yield; some years after, when Col. A. M. Waddell[57] was our mayor, he sent a crew around here to cut down the trees on our Fifth Street side, saying it had been surveyed and found necessary to level the sidewalk and to keep the rain water from running down on those back of us—he then had bought and occupied the premises two doors back of us and we were higher than that lot and still are. I rushed out and stopped the workmen, going to the Mayor's office and daring them to lay an axe to those trees at peril of their lives as I'd shoot the first one who laid his axe to the trees! I hadn't a gun or ever tried to fire one, telling them it was impossible for us all to be on a level in this world—if we were higher we would remain so! I saved the trees—several were blown down in a storm years after, but some remain still, grown very large and beautiful. It is impossible to keep grass growing on the plaza around them as this is a regular parking space for the Baptist Church[58] as well as boarding houses around. When we moved into this house it was complete in every detail and furnished from basement to attic. My parents having gone to New York in 1860 to select new furniture, carpets, etc., taking my eldest sister and baby brother Chesley, carrying to nurse him, "Aunt" Betsy Kedar, an old freed mulatto woman, thinking it unwise to take our regular slave nurse as the country was so excited just then on the slavery question. It was a beautiful sight when the new furnishings were all installed supplemented by the antiques used for years in our old home—every floor beautifully carpeted, windows all curtained, and such beautiful new crockery and silver to

---

[57] Alfred Moore Waddell, former Confederate officer and Wilmington's mayor from 1898-1905.
[58] First Baptist Church, NW corner of Market and 5th.

add to our old stock. A few years before, while we were spending the summer at Smithville, now Southport,[59] thieves broke in our old house and stole at least half of the pretty old china set, white with broad gold band, from store-room shelf where it was placed for safety. There are a very few pieces still left and are much prized. Our new breakfast and dinner set was pure white seal scalloped edge; we gave much of it away in later years. Great big platters and turrens [*sic*] were not needed in this depleted family, but I'm using many smaller pieces. My mother especially loved and enjoyed her pretty tea-set, filagreed guilding on pale salmon edge and a lovely flower (colored and gold) in center and on sides of cups and saucers—no two flowers alike. Only two or three pieces of this are missing—all in china cabinet downstairs. The carpets are most all worn out, except those in the double parlors; they are in a good state of preservation as to color but somewhat moth-eaten.[60] The lace curtains have worn out and been replenished but the silk damask window draperies are packed in the old chest in South East attic room.[61] Our dining room and kitchen in those days and many years after, were in the basement,[62] but when my sister Eliza and I were all that were left in this big house we enclosed the end of the back piazza and built a little kitchen and used our library for a dining room and still do, using the basement for storage, except the rooms occupied by the Colonial Dames as an assembly room.[63] The outbuildings on rear of this lot were servants quarters,[64] and a carriage house, built of brick, the interior well furnished; once all the rooms were occupied by our servants, except one large one, on lower floor

---

[59] Brunswick County community near the mouth of the Cape Fear River 26 miles downstream of Wilmington; county seat from 1808-1978.

[60] The carpets on the first floor were originally wall-to-wall wool in the tapestry Wilton technique. The double parlor carpets were in a medallion pattern.
The pattern and colors of the carpet in the family parlor were reproduced in the 1990s and installed on the west side of the first floor and on the first-to-second floor stairs.

[61] The draperies were rehung following Ellen Bellamy's writing and were damaged during the 1972 fire. The front parlor windows were hung with red drapes and the rear parlor with green.

[62] Having the dining room and kitchen in the basement of large houses was a standard practice of the era.

[63] Floor plans of the house and diagrams of the property are reproduced on pages 42-45.

[64] The building was the quarters for the Bellamy house slaves until the end of the Civil War, and afterward housed servants.

that was fitted up for a wash room. This had brick furnace with large iron pot (still there), and clothes closets for rough dry clothes; a room in our basement, front of kitchen, was used as an ironing room; but after the war, when my brother Willie was reading medicine under my father, preparing to go off to medical college, it was fitted up for him and ever since has gone by the name of "The Office." I recall his bringing home the skeleton of a woman he had dissected in New York and one time standing up our ironing board, similar in shape to a coffin lid, and laying the skeleton on it, frightening the servants who passed through! Only two rooms of the outhouse are occupied now. One I rent to a negro man, James Blackwood, for years employed at Sprunt's compress—for a nominal sum—as a protection for the lot, and old Aurelia Burney who for years rented one of the rooms, is still there, too feeble to work and her nephew in the country brings her wood and provisions. She hasn't paid a cent of rent in 4 years—but I haven't the heart to turn her out, just one of my objects of charity. In one of the downstairs rooms there is some of my dear Ellie deRosset's furniture, Louis' portion still stored there;—her other two sons, Robert and Marsden, having removed theirs. The stable with a number of stalls which were once filled not only with our carriage horses but often the ones from the plantation for the night, bringing us wagon loads of provisions from Grovely. It is only used now for storing shelves, counters, show cases, etc., from the store at 113 Market Street when remodelled for a new tenant some time ago, after Mr. C. H. Fore, who had occupied it for a number of years, went out of business. The carriage house opening on 5th Street has been rented as a garage time and time again—now I've let Dr. Smith keep his car there for the past three years. In olden times we kept a cow too—until the city ordinance forbade—the end stall this way was used for that purpose during night and bad weather—milking in the alley and turning her out during the day. The chicken and turkey house, a neat little structure, slatted in front and side, tin roofed, was built in yard this end of stable but so decayed had to be pulled down a few years ago. Big apricot and fig trees between the two buildings yield quantities of luscious fruit. Both dead and gone, now. We had plenty of everything in those days— the plantation such a prolific place! The store room and meat closet were hung with hams galore and at hog-killing-times no end to the fresh meat and sausages—we laid special stress on the Tom Thumb sausages—dried and smoked and kept during rest of year, our favorite dish for Sunday night suppers—and pickled oysters! The Grovely butter was noted. I've never tasted any since like it. We had a large herd of cows and old Aunt Betsy, one of the old slaves and dairy women my father inherited from his father and brought from South Carolina with a large number of others, had a wonderful talent for that work. I well remember her and her beautiful, spotlessly clean dairy—her vessels were all wooden keelers[65] and piggins[66] made of oak by our own cooper and scoured so faithfully with corn shucks, bleached white and white sand washed and kept for the purpose; no soap, a big iron pot always kept boiling outside during the dairy hours. A little dairy or tiny house on stilts was near by, where the women early in morning on way to work in fields would leave their buckets or big gourds to be filled with the surplus milk and carried later by a child to them. Children called for them when the horn blew for dinner at 12 o'clock. Butter milk too was doled out to them—the old skimmed milk fed to the little pigs— I can see the big old wooden churn scoured so white with a dasher moving up and down at a certain pace by Bella, her little granddaughter, until she saw the lumps of butter, then Aunt Betsy would gather it and wash and salt it and set it down and print it in squares with the wooden paddle, each day's supply was kept separate and brought over several times a week—so much we couldn't consume all and as a great favor my mother would let a few of her friends have a pound or two each. After the death of Aunt Betsy, her daughter, Aunt Nancy, took charge, having inherited the "talent" from her mother and a new dairy was built near, in rear of our house.[67] The orchards were also noted—such fruit of all kinds! On either side of a long avenue from the "big gate" to the house were pear trees of all varieties and such luscious strawberries, raspberries, and all kinds of vegetables of every description. All are gone now, and I'm buying by the pound at a ridiculously high price. None of those generations of slaves are left and the descendants of our old overseers and neighbors—the very plain and common folks are now occupying important places in State and society. I remember as a child how impressed I was by the little daughter of our overseer—consuming most of the castor oil![68] Eating

---

[65] Vessel for cooling liquids; a shallow tub used for household purposes; a milk or cheese tub.
[66] A small wooden pail with one stave longer than the others to serve as a handle.
[67] She was speaking of Grovley Plantation in Brunswick County.

it on her bread! It was kept in a room in the house with all kinds of medicine to be doled out to the sick negroes. Those times were very different! The old plantation,[69] of about 10,000 acres, is still owned by my mother's heirs—although she requested it sold after her death and equally divided. As there was no offer, even at a sacrifice, my brother thought best to sell off the valuable timber from which more was realized and divided. Not being on the highway and the last few miles bad road, makes the land undesirable though it is wonderfully fertile, and has fine game. It is right on Town Creek which empties into Cape Fear River. In olden times all the wood and much of the produce as well as rosin and turpentine was brought to Wilmington on flats. The houses over there all burnt down, even our dwelling—only one little cottage, built a few years ago on that site, has been occupied by first one and another as a guard or keeper for the place. How I loved it as a child. I remember so well our dwelling house—no stately mansion but comfortable and pleasant in a big yard between two lovely magnolias and a long row of Lombardy poplars in front. We usually spent the months of May and June there; no later as it was not considered healthy late in summer, being on the creek, and we would then go to Salem[70] or some higher climate. The upper floor of the house was one tremendous large room with a number of beds and cots innumerable—my grandmother's whole family would occupy that and often other guests with them. Our family lived altogether down stairs—the back piazza enclosed as a dining room—the upstairs steps in one corner and on top of steps leading to yards were marks cut which always told us the noon hour.[71] The fruit was in its glory—and I would follow my father in the orchard culling the most choice which he always deposited in front of mother. He wanted the very best for her; he was always the most devoted husband and his love and attention never failed to the very end, although married fifty-seven years. He was always so solicitous of her health and happiness; he stayed at home closely but would insist upon her going to any social function when invited and excusing him to the host and have a good time and telling him all about it when

---

[68] Castor oil often was used as a laxative.
[69] Grovely
[70] There have been numerous Salems in the state; it is not known to which of them she refers.
[71] Possibly a sort of sun dial.

she got home. My father died August 30, 1896, my mother eleven years after on Oct. 18, 1907. Oh, how bereft we felt with both gone! We missed them both a long time and our hands seemed too empty. Until my sister Eliza's death eight years ago, Jan. 13, 1929, we lived happily together, usually having someone in our rooms across the hall as a protection and company. But since God took this last sister away so suddenly—almost "in the twinkling of an eye," I have been so lonely! Since her death five others near and dear to me have been snatched away—first my nephew, John D. Jr., in March 1932; then on July 16, 1933, my precious Ellie, my first name-sake—Ellen Douglas Bellamy! She was more like my own child than a niece. I was so proud of her and she was my first thought always. I was young and silly and I recall how disgusted my friends and escorts were when they called for me in the hack, the morning after she was born, to go with them on a picnic to the sound, we had planned, when I backed out, preferring to stay home with the baby! She was always a comfort and pleasure to me and it almost broke my heart when God called her away. That very same day James Verner, my niece's husband, of whom I was very fond, died very suddenly—almost instantly. Not quite one year after, May 17, 1934, Lilly, my brother Rob's wife whom I loved very much, died from the effects of a fall a year or more before. That same year, on Nov. 27, 1933, John D. Bellamy, II, another beloved nephew, died—and just one year ago, June 17, 1936 my very precious Ellen Taylor of Columbia, S.C., another namesake, died very suddenly. The news was such a shock to me. I was looking forward to a visit from her in a week or two. I mustn't forget to mention the death of my very faithful,—really beloved servant, Susanna James, an uneducated black negro but so good and fond of me, July, 1935. Two months ago my brother George's wife, Katie T., died, May 1937. But I must not dwell on these sad happenings and try to make the most of what little time is left me here. So will return to old times and tell what I remember of them. The War was my special topic but expect I've told enough about that. The year after the War broke out we had a terrible scourge of yellow fever here in 1862. It became an epidemic in August or September and many fled— our family among them. Many of those who remained were victims of it. One of our most beloved physicians, Dr. James H. Dickson, who was also an elder in our church and old Mr. Green (greatgrandfather of Lizzie Cotchet Metts) and Uncle Northrop (grandfather of Mary and Lizzie May). He was urged by his family to leave but wanted to remain and look after the workmen at his sawmill. His wife, Susan, hearing of his illness, left her family in Marion, S C., where they were staying with Aunt Kitty Taylor (her sister) and came down to him. He died the next day and she returned to Marion and was stricken in a few days after and died. Strange to say no other cases were contracted from her, although the clothes she wore and bedding were stolen from the line where they were hung in a vacant lot nearby—Cousin Susan Rankin also died with it, at Smithville (now Southport) at the home of her father, Mr. John Brown. Her brother, Robert Brown, died on shipboard with yellow fever coming from Nassau. His remains were brought home and then beside Cousin Susan other members of the family died from it—his wife and another sister, Mrs. Carrie Prioleau and her young son, Thomas. It was thought it was brought here by steamers running the blockade.

Aug. 6, 1937—It has been quite a while since I have written any on my memoirs—and I recall that today is the 116th anniversary of my dear mother's birth, so hard for me to realize she passed away from us October, 1907, nearly 30 years ago, aged 86—so remarkable for her age in mind and health although for the last few years she was unable to walk without her crutches—her knees having become drawn from rheumatism. It was such a privilege for my sister and me to watch and wait on her and how much did we miss her! August 1937—Last month my niece (and a most precious one), Elize Verner,[72] paid me a sweet little visit which was cut short by a wire from her son in Columbia announcing the birth of twins to his wife—a girl and a boy—Elize's first grand children—the girl named for her and the boy for its father, James S. Verner, Jr. So you can't wonder she is proud of them! Thus, the eternal thread of life is woven!

---

[72] Born Eliza Bellamy Duffie, first child of Belle Bellamy and William Jefferson Duffie.

DESCRIPTION OF BELLAMY HOME
March 9, 1939

It has been suggested by my friends that I write a description of my home, 503 Market Street, and add to my Memoirs which I began to write April, 1937, now nearly two years ago.[73] As I may have already said, this lot on North East corner of 5th and Market Streets was purchased by my father from Mr. James McCumber, Sr.,[74] in the fall of 1858 and excavation for foundation soon begun. Mr. McCumber could only be induced to sell part of his lots reserving the one next door which was bought from his heirs nearly 40 years later by my brother, Robert R. Bellamy, who built the house now standing on it into which he with his wife and only son, Hargrove, moved Dec. 1896.[75] On the extreme corner of this lot there was a little grocery shop and two little cottages which were all pulled down and used for fire wood. The basement of this house is about four feet underground but with a broad area running all around insuring it against dampness.[76] Solid brick pillars are placed at intervals to support the columns above; heavy brick walls are between all four large rooms. The dining room was the front northwest[77] corner and back of that the breakfast room or "pantry" as it was then called, with lockers below and glass cases extending to the ceiling all across one side. A fire place was in that room, while in the dining room there was a grate, and marble mantels in both.[78] Back of this room is a large store room with shelves and lockers below. On the other side of a broad hall or passage, the front room was called the ironing room—washing being done in the wash room in the servants house in the back yard. A fire place was in the ironing room. Back of that was the large kitchen with lockers on one

---

[73] Diagrams of the property and floor plans of the buildings are reproduced on pages 42-45.

[74] Brothers Robert S. and James N. McCumber sold the lot, just over a half-acre, to Bellamy by deed recorded July 28, 1859 for $4500 (New Hanover County Deed Book, QQ, p. 77). There was a new wooden house on the lot in 1849 when it was insured for $500. In 1853 it again was insured, this time for $800 (New Hanover County Deed Books, FF, p. 420 and KK, p. 392).

[75] The Robert R. Bellamy House at 509 Market Street burned about 1982. The parking lot for Bellamy Mansion now occupies the site.

[76] She is writing about the Bellamy's house.

[77] Actually the southwest corner.

[78] The mantels actually are made of slate and painted or marbelized to resemble marble.

side with shelves and doors; on other side just a long locker shelf with shut-in places beneath for pots and large cooking utensels. There was a large built in cooking range more suitable for a hotel but we had a large family with big appetites—besides the negro servants, nine of them living on lot and fed from our kitchen. In one corner of kitchen was a large sink with a big copper boiler, water heated from range, as was the case with but very few houses—water pipes and bath room—hot and cold water and shower bath. The water was supplied by a large cistern in yard and pumped up by a force pump on back area through pipes to a large oak-covered, zinc lined tank in a room on floor in back of attic. It was the duty of Guy, our butler, to pump and fill that tank first thing every morning. On other side of back area under the winding steps that led up to next was a meat closet usually kept filled with hams and bacon from the bountiful supply from Grovely Plantation ten miles across the river in Brunswick County. At the extreme back middle of area a door and steps leading down into a big coal pit under back steps which held ten to fifteen tons of coal thrown down through a chute covered by a heavy iron disc in yard, foot of steps. The ceiling to basement rooms was high and windows so arranged to let in all the light and air. The floor above, or main parlor floor was beautifully finished off—high ceiling,[79] ornamental[80] cornices all around ceiling—just 4 rooms on that floor. The sitting room, southwest corner, the library back of that, beautiful marble mantels, black[81]—while across the broad hall were the double parlors, folding doors between,[82] elaborately decorated plaster walls all done by negro plasterers born and raised on Grovely—beautiful white marble mantels—large double windows to the floor, front and back, with two windows on side of both rooms—beautiful elaborate gas chandeliers in both rooms bronze and gold, with six lights with pretty glass shades[83]. Massive gilt[84] cornices were over each window from which hung the heavy silk brocaded damask curtains and lambrequins—two shades

---

[79] 11 feet, 9 inches
[80] Plaster.
[81] The mantels actually are made of slate and painted or marbelized to resemble marble.
[82] The dividing doors are sliding pocket doors.
[83] The gasoliers throughout the house were manufactured by Cornielius and Baker of Philadelphia.
[84] The cornices actually are thin sheets of brass hammered over an ornate mold and applied to wooden forms.

of red in front parlor—green and gold in the back one, with heavy double sliding—doors between the rooms practically throwing the two into one large room. Elegant heavily gilt-framed mirrors are over each mantle [*sic.*] piece—both rooms alike, all furniture having mahogany frames and done up in beautiful red silk damask—a sofa and four large stuffed arm-chairs, four smaller and four little reception chairs—piano, stool to piano in back room. Beautiful oil paintings on walls are the work of my sister, Mary E. Bellamy while a student at Barhamville, near Columbia, S.C. And while there she was impressed by the beauty of the Clarkson home on corner of Bull and Blanding Streets, which was burnt by Sherman not very long after, and as my father was contemplating building this house she made a drawing of it and assisted Mr. Rufus Bunnell, the architect,[85] in modelling this after that manner. But to return to the parlors; since I have been a "shuit-in" [*sic.*] upstairs they are never used, but are just a show place which my companion, Miss Stallings, takes great pride in exhibiting to strangers visiting the city. The carpets while moth eaten some are wonderfully preserved, the colors still bright and fresh—large medalion in middle, beautiful bunches of flowers on white ground with borders shaded reds all around. The broad hall or passage has a wide staircase, twenty-one steps, with mahogany rail and newell posts, a beautiful velvet carpet held by broadsilver rods, and the hall covered with a velvet carpet to match.[86] Large back door with glass lights above and on sides—The front door was and still is so much admired; very large heavy, with wood panels; on the outside is a big rosette or wood-work ornament, heavy silver knocker, lock and doorbell knob. Above the door a carved glass[87] beautifully flowered and on each side three panels of glass—the top curved, of ground glass with a vine of carved grapes and leaves. The gas chandelier front hall is very pretty—has three lights. The chandeliers in the sitting room and library are very attractive too; they are bronze and gilt, beautifully moulded, a little boy on each arm blowing a horn, etc. Upstairs the bedroom floor is divided very much the same way excepting a small room in front of hall and a large bath room on northwest side, entered from that back bedroom and another

---

[85] Rufus Bunnell of Connecticut was a young draftsman employed by the building's architect, James F. Post.
[86] The hall was refloored with oak parquet, perhaps about 1896 when Robert R. Bellamy built his house next door, at 509 Market Street.
[87] Actually etched glass.

door on back piazza. Very large closets are between rooms on East side while those between rooms on west side are smaller.[88] The west rooms are larger and there is communication between rooms on both sides and a pretty little balcony in front of both rooms overlooking the spacious porch or piazza downstairs, which extends around front and both sides over ten feet wide with banister—with fourteen massive fluted columns, their heavy bases resting on the brick pillars below. The columns, over two feet in diameter, are of Grecian architecture, Corinthian style. On these the roof rests extending over all—a great protection from heavy rains. The front steps are wide and heavy extending from one pillar to another, having broad curved bannisters with large square carved posts. On the ground is a large window[89] on back westside connecting the porch that runs across the whole back and terminates in a winding staircase with door at top to be locked at night for protection. The windows on bedroom floor are just above ones downstairs; the ones in front extending to floor leading out to a balcony. The tops of these windows are arched beautifully but hard for fitting curtains. The "attic" or 4th floor above this is divided very much the same way except the hall is wider making rooms a little smaller, but very comfortable—bedrooms with a large dressing room adjoining back rooms—one of these the "tank" room. These rooms were occupied later by members of our large family—but the two front rooms inside were used as lumber rooms. At the front of hall there is a raised platform over front porch which I used as a "doll house" as a child, and later for neighborhood charades. Above that is the cupola or observatory,[90] quite a good sized room, glass windows on all four sides, giving a good view of the city. The staircase leading to that is quite as good as the ones below. I have tried to describe the house to give an idea to future generations of its beauty which is generally recognized by strangers visiting the city, many of them asking admission; but we have to be careful who we let come in. Some of these days business may extend up this way and the house pulled down to make room for stores, banks, etc., as was the case on Front Street. I can

---

[88] The existence of closets in 18th and 19th century houses often is questioned or said to be a sign of great wealth. That is not the case. Closets often were built as original features of larger houses.
[89] This actually is a false window, with louvered blinds.
[90] Technically known as a belvedere, meaning beautiful view, it was designed so that when its windows were open, rising hot air escaped, cooling the house.

remember when that was the principal residential section from the railroad down to Castle Street. On Red Cross near East side of Front, there was a handsome brick house with white marble trimming and steps owned by Mr. James Grist and occupied by him and family but they later moved back to Washington, N.C., from whence they came. Three of my sisters-in-law and a number of my other kin descended from that same Grist family. When I was a child, our Pastor and wife (Rev. M. B. Greer) lived in that house awhile and I often visited them. Next came the old Flanner home. The street was thickly built up, but I only mention the most important. Coming down on next comer was the Frank Brown residence. Then Dr. James Dickson, who was in 1862 one of the yellow fever victims and his office a small building in same yard. Then came Dr. Freeman's place, a homeopathic[91] doctor. And then the handsome P. K. Dickinson home, corner Front and Chestnut, a beautiful house built high up, far back from street—lovely garden—grand magnolias and other evergreens, a most imposing place. He, by the way, was the great, great grandfather of my grand nephews, Robert, Marsden and Louis H. deRosset, sons of my beloved niece and namesake, Ellen Douglas, daughter of my brother Marsden. Their father, Robert Cowan deRosset's grandmother, Eliza, being a daughter of Mrs. P. K. Dickinson who as the widow of Mr. Robert Cowan, lived in that home with another widowed sister, Mrs. Walker. His mother, Jane Dickinson Cowan, married Louis Henry deRosset. He and a sister, Kate, who married W. Dougald McMillan, 3rd, were their only children; but he was married before, his first wife, Marie Finley, of Charleston, S.C., was a young woman of French descent and they had one daughter, Gabriel, who married Alfred Waddell, and was his third wife. But I'm not recording geneology only mentioning those connected with our family. Coming on down, on next corner was a handsome brick house, home of the Meares family and next Mr. Eli Hall's, not so handsome, some of them wooden. On corner of that block was the bank building, with the Walkers occupying back and upper story. Middle of next block a fine brick residence owned and occupied by Gilbert Potter and family—father of Mrs. Edward Kidder who lived on corner of 3rd and Dock. Corner Front and Market, a

---

[91] A system of medical practice that treats a disease especially by the administration of minute doses of a remedy that would, in healthy persons, produce symptoms similar to those of the disease.

brick building and the Commercial Hotel. On next block a few small buildings then on corner of Dock the old Hill home and then the Bradleys' and next, a very nice home occupied by the Leobs,[92] fashionable dressmakers. Then came the Presbyterian Church of which I've written already a description. The old "Session House" still stands in rear of a store built on that lot.[93] Next corner of Orange is the old Dr. Anderson home still standing. The Baptist Church was on corner of Ann Street, on high hill which washed away, so the church was condemned and pulled down.[94] They worshipped in City Hall 'till their church on opposite corner from me, 5th and Market, was completed enough to occupy, though the steeple was not finished 'till some years after. It was started soon after this house.[95] We watched the workmen on the steeple raising those round brass balls—the largest one as big as a barrel! On opposite side of Front Street, coming from R. R., were a number of nice buildings, the most imposing being between Mulberry (afterwards changed to Grace St.) and Chestnut. There was the Cowan home. The Pearce and the James Dawson home on corners—way back in yard, later used as Cape Fear Club until they built the present club house on old Bettencourt lot, southeast corner 2nd and Chestnut; the Murchison Bank is now there. On next corner, coming South, where the Southern Building now stands,[96] was Dr. James McCrea's home; an old tall building right on the street, with upper piazzas. The Lawtons' occupied it and Mr. Lawton had his furniture factory there—he designed and made several of our old bureaus and bedsteads. Later this building was occupied by the Lumsdens as an ice-cream parlor and a dressmaking establishment by Mrs. Lumsden (the former Mrs. Lawton) and her sister, Mrs. Brock. Next to that, on corner Front and Princess—the heads of the old Anderson family lived in a handsome

---

[92] Loebs
[93] It since has been demolished.
[94] Historians believe that the church still stands as a dwelling known as Baptist Hill, 305 South Front Street.
[95] First Baptist Church is the design of Philadelphia architect, Samuel Sloan who also designed the 1859 First Presbyterian Church.
[96] The Southern Building on the SW corner of Front and Chestnut streets, was designed by Charles McMillen and demolished about 1968 to make way for the North Carolina National Bank. John D. Bellamy, Jr. and his sons, William McKoy and Emmett Hargrove, had their law office in the Southern Building.

old house with a large garden. (Now the site of the Peoples Bank)[97]. Just next below old Mrs. Anderson (towards the river), her daughter, Mrs. Washington Davis, lived but later moved next to her brother, Dr. Anderson, on Orange Street next to Front. On next block, about the middle, was the Bank building, "'Commercial Bank," but after the war used as the National Bank—and on corner of Market, the Drug Store operated by McLin—still standing but remodelled, for years owned by Robt. McKoy but later owned by my brother Robert and run by him for years but now occupied as Toms Drug Store, but owned by my nephew, Hargrove Bellamy, who now runs the wholesale Drugs, Second and Market, business inherited from his father. Across the corner, the old brick building still stands, occupied by a number of different merchants and now by Finklestein—Next below that on Front was my grandfather Harriss' office, in olden times, still standing and owned by my brother Robert's son, Hargrove. Then on Front to Castle many old buildings, viz.: old Leamn's home, the Market House, built later after giving up old market house in middle of street extending from Front to Water. In the tower of Market House was the old bell rung by a negro woman owned by the Gilberts; first in morning, the breakfast bell; an hour later the "Turn Out," or school bell; same at dinner time and at 9 at night rung again, after which servants or slaves were not allowed in street without passes from their owners. There were other buildings, only a few left now and they remodelled. An old sailor boarding-house[98] is now the laundry; the house on Front and Nun now owned and occupied by Lawrence Sprunt (who inherited it from his father, James Sprunt), much altered from time to time, was originally Gov. Dudley's home and owned by the Dudleys. He was great grandfather of Annie Dudley who married my aunt's son, Willie H. Howell. I have told enough of this, but maybe it may be of interest in years to come. No doubt I've repeated many things, but I really haven't the strength or patience to read it over. I don't claim to be a ready writer! This is new business for me!

April 12, 1939, Wed.—In connection with the description of this house I must tell of a "Party" or "Housewarming" my parents gave

---

[97] Peoples Bank, also designed by Samuel Sloan of Philadelphia, was replaced by the current Wachovia Bank building in 1959.
[98] Seamen's Bethel, on the southwest corner of Front and Dock streets, now demolished.

soon after moving in our new home, pronounced the grandest party ever given in Wilmington! It was complimentary to two bridal couples in our family connection—Cousin Hattie Taylor, only daughter of Uncle Taylor and Aunt Kitty, who lived in their handsome marble home now used as the Light Infantry Armory[99] on next block, a few doors below us. She married Dr. Edward S. Tennent, of Charleston, S. C., the wedding taking place in the large pillard[100] room on East side. He was a surgeon in Confederate Army; one and a half years later he died from a fatal wound in battle in Marion, S.C., where the family was refugeeing, leaving 1 little boy, Edward, Jr., a few weeks old. He, by the way, died in Spartanburg. S.C.—his mother preceeding him several years. He left a wife and two grown children both fine and good. The other bridal couple was my Uncle George Harriss and Julia, daughter of Mr. John A. Landers of Elm Grove, four miles from here. I can remember how beautiful everything was, especially the long table set in dining room laden with everything conceivably good! Hot food and drink brought on from the kitchen across the hall. My father being such a strict temperance man, would have no cocktails (unheard of in those days but now an introduction to every feast) or any strong drink, not even wine—but plenty of coffee, tea and chocolates, etc. The end of back piazza was enclosed with blinds and there sat a band which discoursed delightful music all during the evening. That was in March 1861—the weddings having taken place Feb. 20th and 27th The war actually broke out April 12th and ended all entertaining for four long years.

Later—April 23rd, 1940—I have written this for fear some of these days this old home might be burned or pulled down to be replaced by business houses or something else. Bobby Little, aged 15, son of my very dear friends, Fred and Bessie Little, now living on 17th and Chestnut Street, has kindly agreed to typewrite this for me—several copies—which I'll give to those nearest and dearest who I think will value and preserve it, in case mine should be lost or destroyed. I'll not attempt to write more as I'm so old and rather feeble. Should I live till

---

[99] The building was later used as the library, a city office and now staff offices for First Baptist Church.
[100] Billard room.

May 11, 1940[101] I will celebrate my 88th birthday. I have been "shut-in" now for over 9 years, upstairs, not able to get up and down steps and now I'm just regaining my strength from a serious illness about Christmas time. I can walk from room to room and am able to enjoy my friends who are so kind and attentive and help me to while away many lonely hours—and above all, God is so good to me, giving me so many blessings and comforts and letting me keep my mind unimpaired, my hearing as well as ever and my sight sufficient for all that is necessary. I have a very faithful and kind companion, Miss Lina Stallings, who has been with me nine years.

Goodbye now, one and all. If we do not see each other again in this world, I pray we may all meet "Beyond the River where the Surges cease to Roll."

ELLEN DOUGLAS BELLAMY.

---

[101] She did; Ellen Bellamy died January 30, 1946.

Dr. and Mrs. John D. Bellamy family

John Dillard Bellamy, MD TO: **Eliza McIlhenny Harriss Bellamy**
b. September 18, 1817   b. August 6, 1821
d. August 30, 1896   d. October 18, 1907

Children:

Mary Elizabeth (Belle) Bellamy
b. November 27, 1840
d. January 7, 1900

Marsden Bellamy
b. January 14, 1843
d. December 1, 1909

William James Harriss (Willie) Bellamy, MD
b. September 16, 1844
d. November 18, 1911

Eliza Bellamy
b. June 8, 1846
d. January 13, 1929

Ellen Douglas Bellamy
b. May 11, 1852
d. January 30, 1946

John Dillard Bellamy, Jr.
b. March 24, 1854
d. September 25, 1942

George Harriss Bellamy
b. April 24, 1856
d. March 14, 1924

Kate Taylor Bellamy
b. June 19, 1858
d. July 14, 1858

Chesley Calhoun Bellamy
b. September 29, 1859
d. August 7, 1881

Robert Rankin Bellamy
b. July 21, 1861
d. April 7, 1926

BASEMENT

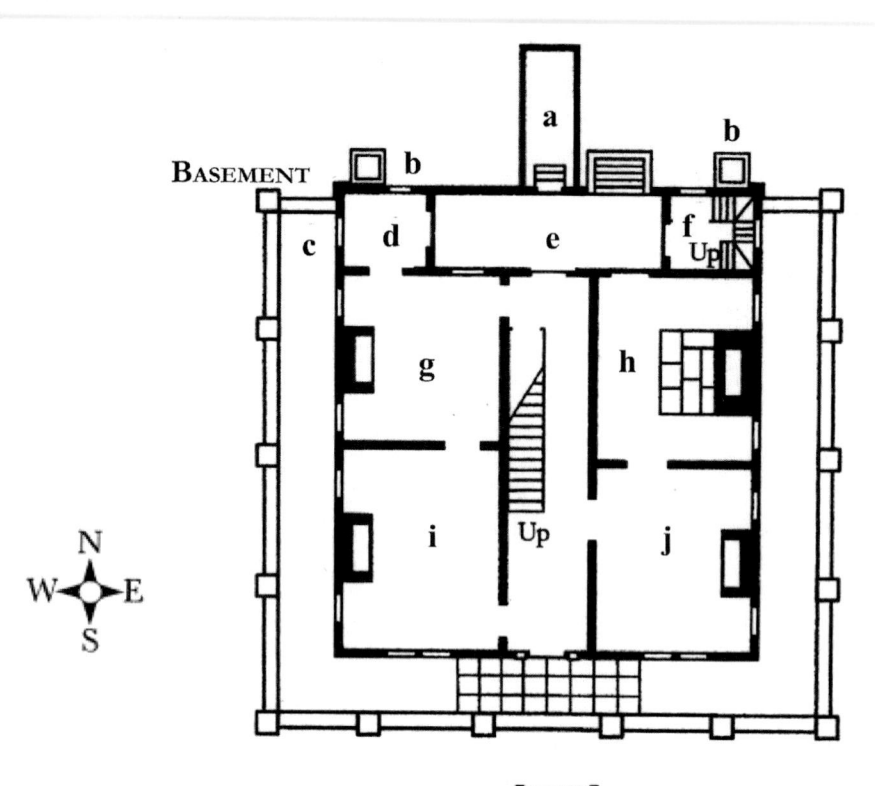

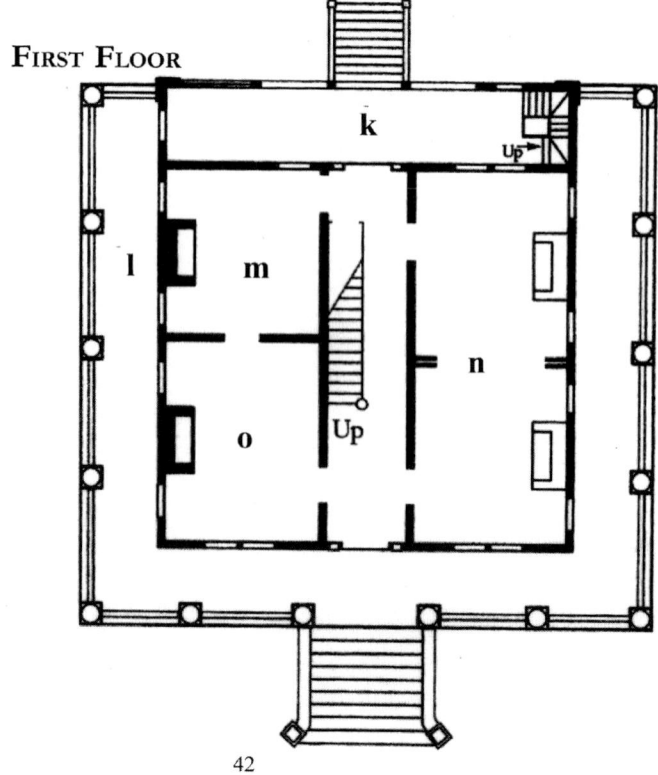

FIRST FLOOR

42

Floorplan of the Bellamy Manison

Second Floor

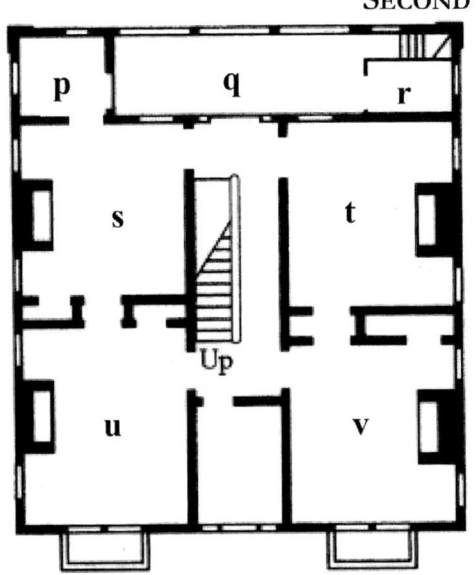

a Coal cellar
b Downspout catch basin
c Area way
d Scullery
e Work area
f Meat closet
g Butler's pantry
h Kitchen
i Dining room
j Ironing room
k First floor back porch
l Piazzas (porches)
m Library
n Double parlors
o Family parlor
p Bathroom
q Upper back porch
r Porch bathroom
   (installed circa 1900)
s t u v Bedrooms
w Water tank room
x Lumber room
   (18th & 19th century
   term for storage area)
y z aa bb Children's
   bedrooms
cc "Play stage"
   (interior area over front
   porch used as play stage
   by the children)
dd Belvedere

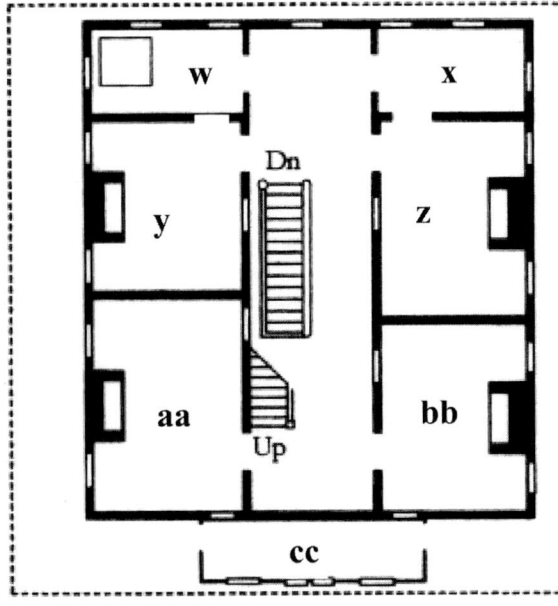

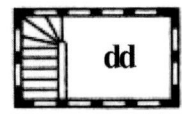

Third Floor

Belvedere

43

Bellamy Mansion Property Diagram

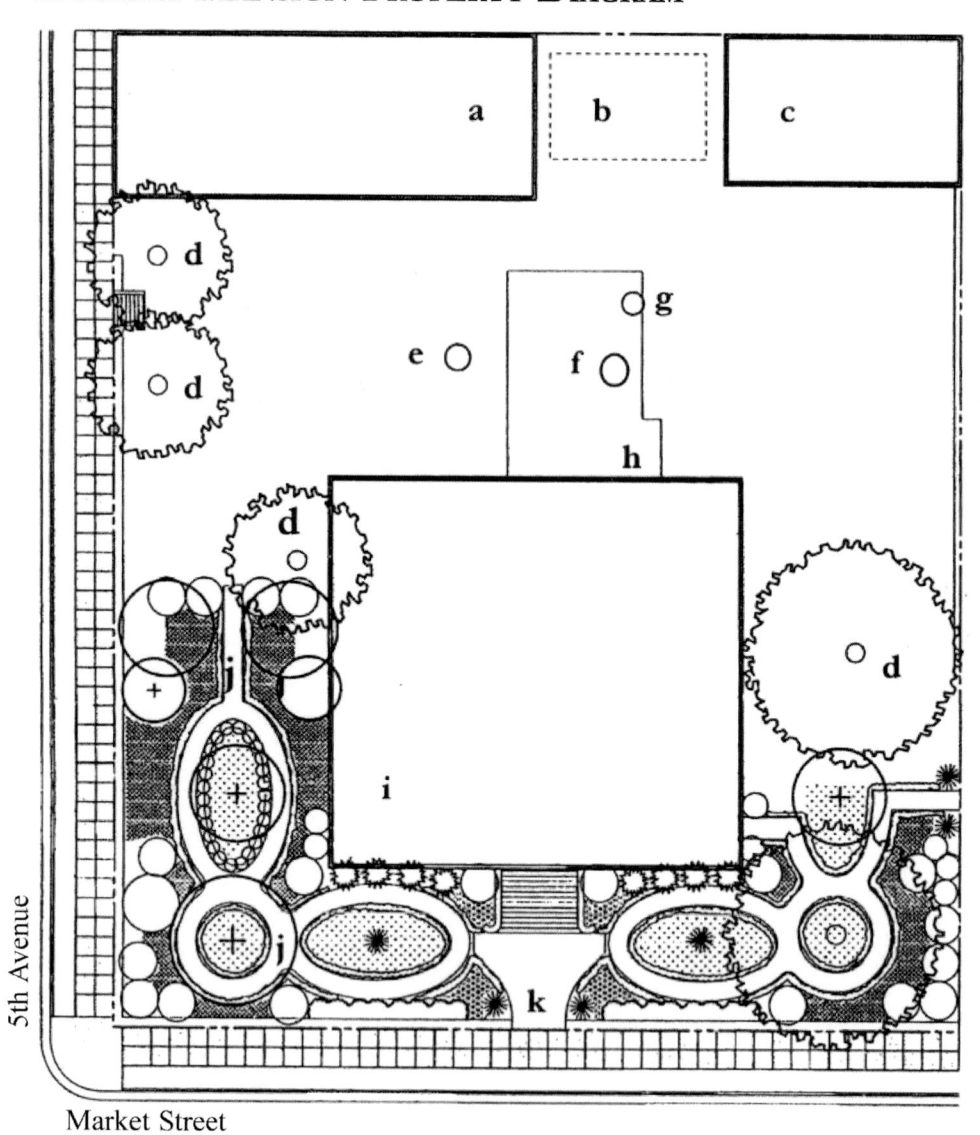

a

b

c

d

d

e

g

f

h

d

d

j

i

j

k

5th Avenue

Market Street

N
W E
S

In 1866, the City of Wilmington widened 5th Avenue and Market Street, consequently the size of the west lawn was reduced by 19' and the depth of the front lawn shrank by 6'. Apparently, the City's decision caught Dr. Bellamy unaware. Construction had already begun on a new brick wall with ornate cast iron fencing that was to border the 5th and Market sides of the property. The fence work was halted and the plan was altered to accommodate the enlargement of the public right of way. It's likely that the property was landscaped shortly after the fencing project was completed. The formal gardens were created in the front and side yards while all indication suggest that the back of the house was essentially a working space with a small poultry yard and some fruit and fig trees. The earliest dated photograph of the house, taken early in 1873, indicated that formal plantings were already well established by that time. Bellamy family tradition suggests that Mrs. Bellamy was an aficionado of wild flowers and that she kept a notebook on her botanical interests. Unfortunately, this notebook never has been discovered.

Excerpt from "Historic Landscaping at the Bellamy Mansion,"
North Carolina Preservation, Summer 1995
by Jonathan Noffke
Director of the Bellamy Mansion 1993-2000

a   Carriage house
b   Poultry shed
c   Slave quarters
d   Magnolia grandiflora
e   Cistern
f   Grate to coal storage
g   Well
h   Brick paved area
i   Mansion
j   Oyster shell paths surrounding elliptical & circular beds
k   Front gate

Landscape Illustration by Matt Langston,
Boney Architects, Wilmington, NC

Part of Gray's Map, Wilmington, North Carolina, 1881

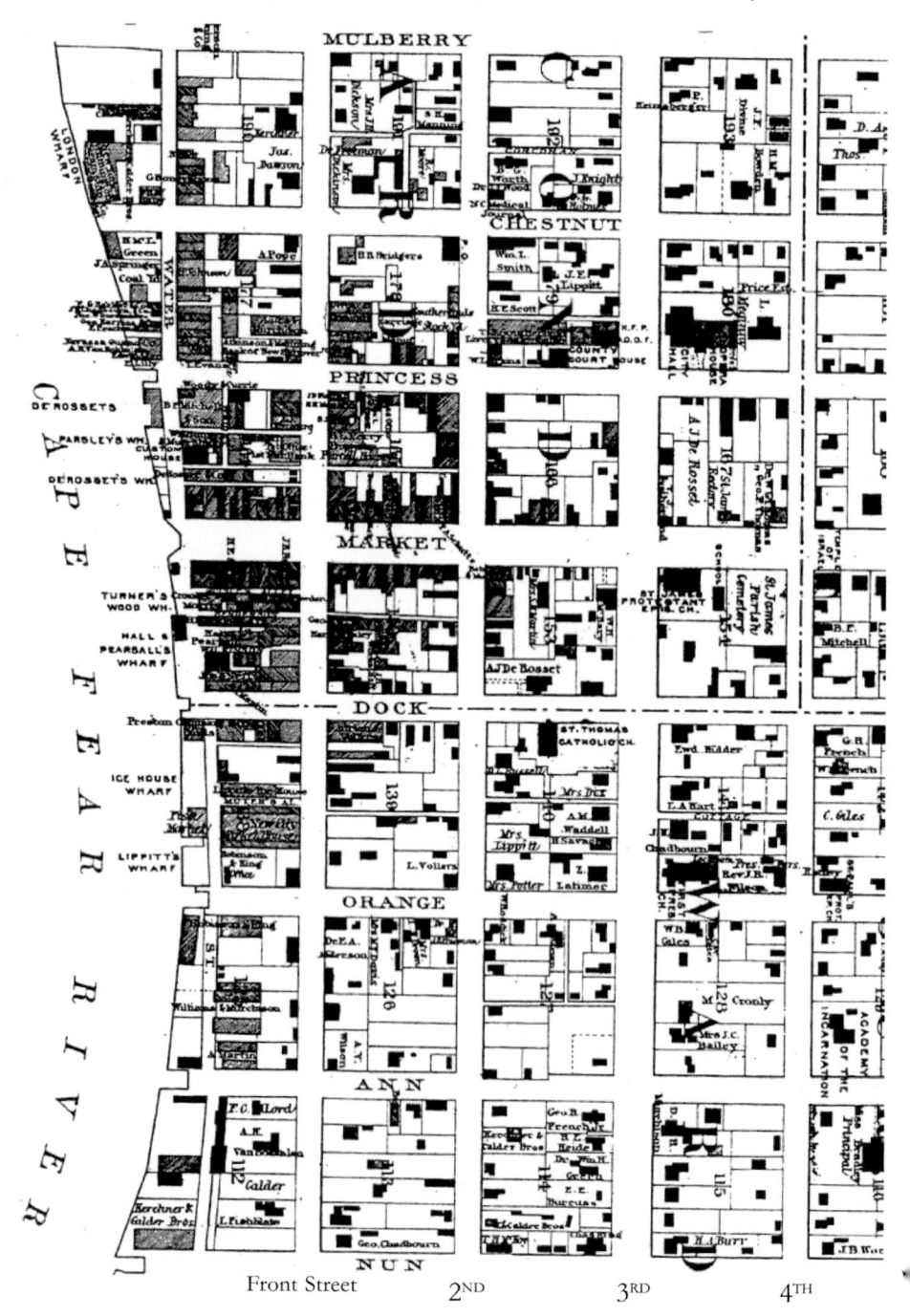

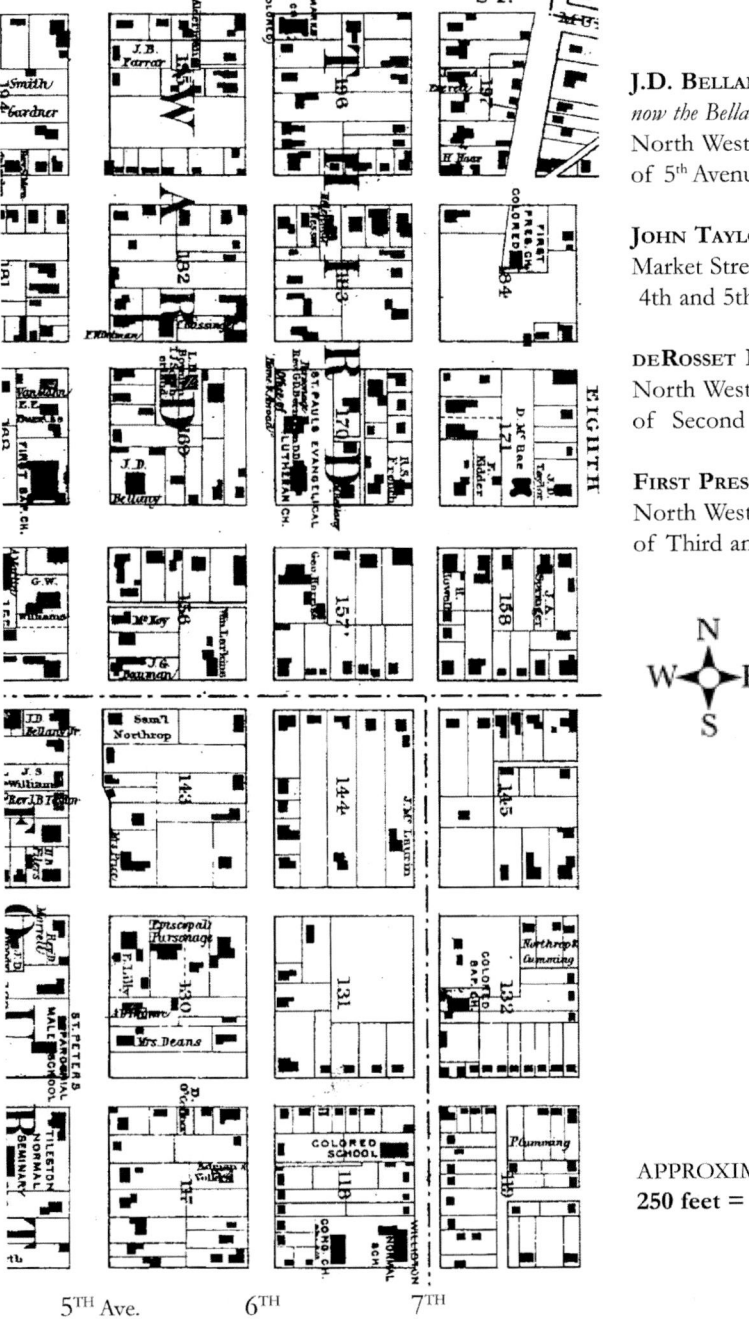

J.D. Bellamy House,
now the Bellamy Mansion
North West Corner
of 5th Avenue and Market Street

John Taylor House
Market Street between
4th and 5th Streets

deRosset House
North West Corner
of Second and Dock Streets

First Presbyterian Church
North West Corner
of Third and Orange Streets

APPROXIMATE SCALE:
250 feet = 1 inch

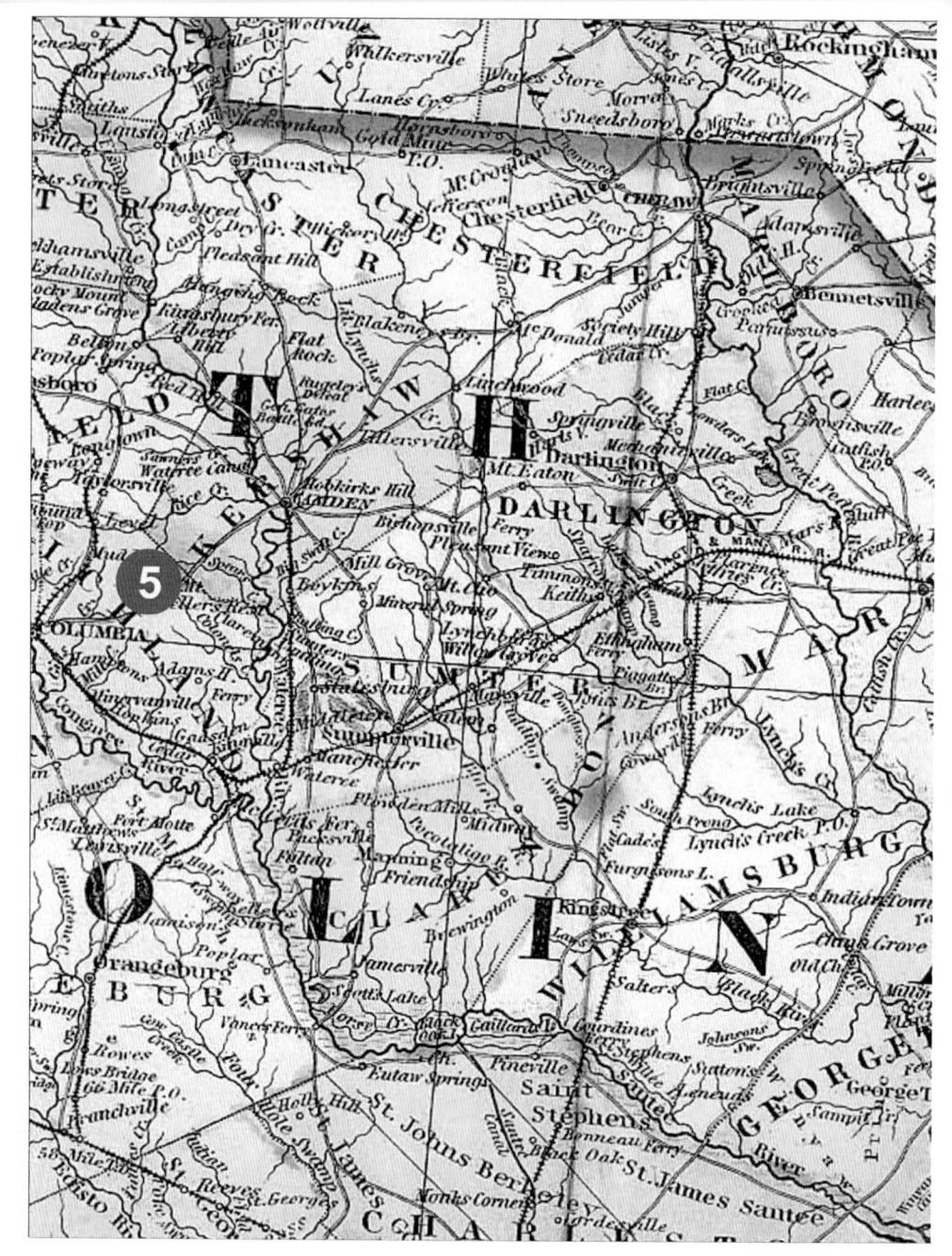

SOUTH CAROLINA

NORTH CAROLINA

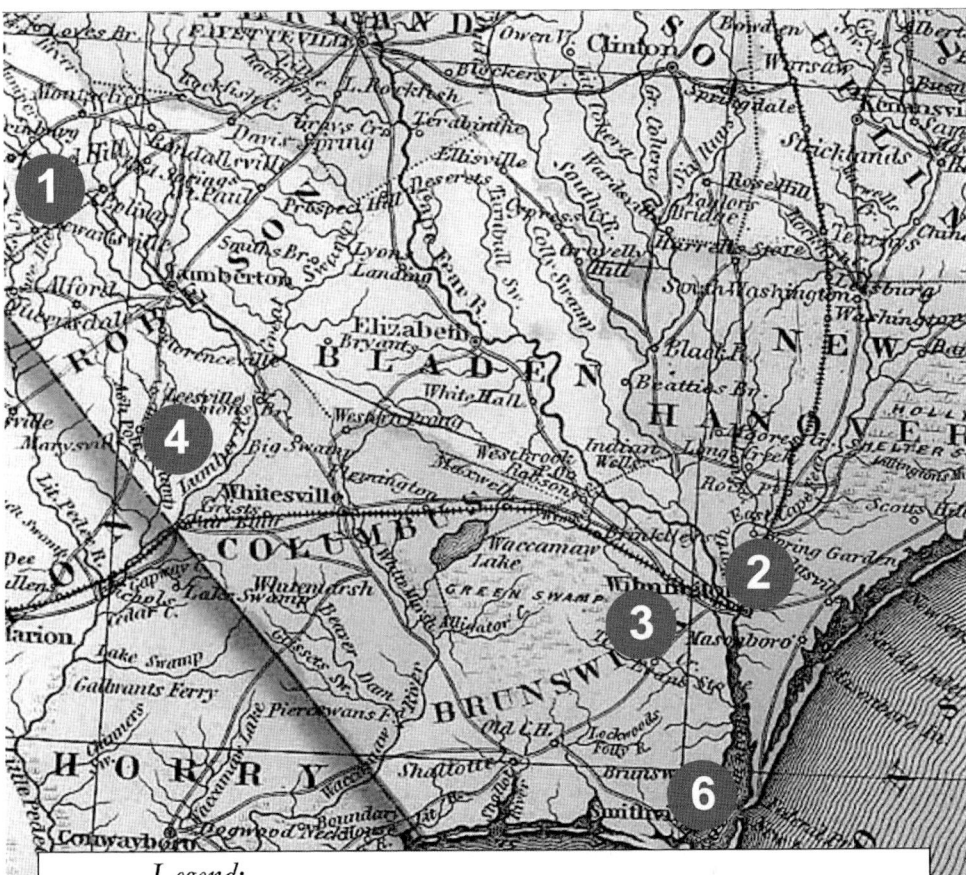

Legend:

1. FLORAL COLLEGE, site of college for women where the Bellamy family took refuge during the Civil War.

2* WILMINGTON, site of Dr. John D. Bellamy's home located at 503 Market Street.

3* GROVELY PLANTATION, site of Dr. John D. Bellamy's plantation where the family fled during the Union occupation of Wilmington.

4* CHADBOURN, formerly known as Grist, site of Dr. John D. Bellamy's turpentine operation.

5* BARHAMVILLE, site of Mary Elizabeth (Belle) Bellamy's finishing school just north of Columbia, South Carolina.

6 SOUTHPORT (formerly Smithville)

* These sites were located along the east-west route of the Wilmington & Manchester Railroad.

Johnson's Map, North and South Carolina, 1861   Scale: 1 inch equals 25 miles
courtesy New Hanover County Public Library's Local History Room

INDEX

A
Alford family, 9
Alligator, 14, 15
Anderson, Dr., House, 37, 38

B
Bank Building, 37
Bank of Cape Fear, IX
Barhamville School, 21, 22, 34
Bell ringing, 38
Bella (enslaved dairywoman's granddaughter), 28
Bellamy House, IX, 3, 4, 24, 32-35, 42, 43
Bellamy House, floor plan, 42, 43
Bellamy House, furnishings, 11, 25, 26
Bellamy House, landscaping, 24, 25
Bellamy House, property diagram, 44-45
Bellamy, Chesley C. (brother), 19, 25, 41
Bellamy, Dr. John D. (father), IX, X, XI, 6-9, 11, 14-18, 28-30, 39, 41
Bellamy, Dr. William James (brother), 8, 9, 15, 16, 19, 20, 27, 41
Bellamy, Eliza Harriss (mother), IX, 6-9, 11, 13, 17, 20, 23, 25, 28-31, 41
Bellamy, Eliza (sister), 16, 17, 19, 26, 30, 41
Bellamy, Ellen D. (niece), 18, 30, 36
Bellamy, Ellen Douglas, VII, VIII, XI, X, IX, 3, 4, 8, 10, 12-14,16, 18-22, 24-31, 39, 40-41
Bellamy, George Harriss (brother), 8, 16, 19, 41
Bellamy, Hargrove (nephew), 19, 32, 38
Bellamy, John D. (brother), 7, 8, 13, 18, 19, 37, 41
Bellamy, John D. (nephew, brother William's son), 30, 37
Bellamy, John D. II (nephew, brother Marsden's son), 30
Bellamy, Kate Taylor (sister), 18, 41
Bellamy, Marguerite (niece), 7
Bellamy, Marsden (brother), 7, 8, 14, 15, 19, 22, 41
Bellamy, Mary Elizabeth (Belle)
 see Duffie, Mrs. Mary
Bellamy, Mrs. Emma Hargrove (sister-in-law), 19
Bellamy, Mrs. Hattie Harllee (sister-in-law), 22
Bellamy, Mrs. Kate Taylor, 30
Bellamy, Mrs. Lily Hargrove (sister-in-law), 19, 30
Bellamy, Robert Rankin (brother), 6, 13, 18, 19, 30, 38, 41
Bellamy, Robert R. (grand nephew), 6
Bellamy, William McKoy (nephew), 37
Bethea family, 9
Betsy (enslaved dairywoman), 28
Bettencourt lot, 37
Blackwood, James (roomer), 27
Blair, Brig. General Francis P. (Union), 9, 11
Boushea family, 12
Bradley House, 37
Brown, T.W. (jeweler), 11
Brown, Frank, House, 36
Bunnell, Rufus (architect), 34
Buchanan, Jane, 19, 20
Burgwin-Wright House, 23
Burney, Aurelia (roomer), 27
Burr, Mrs. Horace, 6
Butter making, 28

C
Cape Fear Club, 37
Caroline (Mrs. Bellamy's maid), 13
Center Presbyterian Church, 9, 19, 21
Chadbourn (Columbus County), 10
City Hall (used for Baptist Services), 37
Clarkson House (Columbia, SC), 34
Colbe, Rev. (Presbyterian), 9, 20
Colonial Dames
 see NC Colonial Dames of America
Commercial Bank, 38
Commercial Hotel, 37
Costin House, 25
Cowan House, 37
Cowan, Platt, 20

D
Davis family, 9, 19
Davis, Mrs. W., House, 38
Dawson, James, House, 37

DeRossett family, 27, 36
Dickenson, P.K., House, 36
Drew, Mrs. (weaver), 14
Drug Store, 38
Dry Pond (gallows site), 23
Dudley House, 38
Duffie, Mrs. Mary Elizabeth (Belle) (sister), 11, 14, 18, 20, 21, 31, 34, 41
Duffie, William (brother-in-law), 18, 21, 22

F
Farthing House, 25
Finklestein store, 38
First Presbyterian Church, Columbia, SC, 21
First Baptist Church, 25, 37
First Presbyterian Church, 5, 23, 24
Flanner House, 36
Flora McDonald College, 20
Floral College, X, XI, 4, 8, 9, 15, 16, 17
Fonvielle, Dr. C.E., XI
Food storage, 13-16
Fore, C.H., 27
Fort Fisher, X, 4, 5, 15
Freeman, Dr. (homopathic), 36
French, G.Z. (Postmaster), 8
Funeral rites, 19

G
Gage, Mrs. (school), 20
Gallows Hill (hanging ground), 22
Gilchrist family, 9
Gilmour, Rev. A.D. (Presbyterian), 24
Greer, Rev. M.B. (Presbyterian), 36
Gregg, Bishop (Episcopalian), 19
Grist House, 36
Grist (Columbus County), 10
Grovely Plantation, 5, 10, 12, 14, 15, 27, 28, 29, 33
Guy (enslaved butler and coachman), 13-15, 33

H
Haley, Dr. John H., VIII
Hall, Eli, House, 36
Harllee, Dr. Robert, 22
Harriss family, 6, 11, 17, 23, 38, 39
Hawley, Brig. Gen. Joseph R. (Union), X, 5, 7
Hawley, Mrs. J.R., 5, 7

Hepburn, Rev. A.D. (Presbyterian), 5
Hewitt, Mr. (shoemaker), 14
Hill, House, 37

J
James, Susanna (servant & friend of Ellen), 30
Jewetts, G.W. (teacher), 8
Joan (enslaved nurse), 13
Johnson, Rev. Daniel (college head), 5

K
Kedar, Betsy (freed nurse), 25
Kenan family (donation to church), 24
Kidder, Mrs. E., House, 37

L
Landers, John A., House, 39
Lawton, Mrs., House, 37
Leamn House, 38
Leary, Sam (Willie's enslaved man servant), 16
Leob House, 37
Light Infantry Armory, 39
Lilly family (shop owners), 9
Little, Bobby (typed manuscript), 39
Lowery, Henry Barry (Robeson County), 16
Lumsden (ice cream parlor & dressmaker), 37

M
MacRae family, 7
MacRae, General Alexander, 16
Market House, 38
112 Market Street, 27
503 Market Street, 4, 22, 32
Marks (principle Barhamville School), 22
Mary Ann (Bellamy slave), 13
Maxton *see Shoe Heel Depot*
McAllister family, 9
McCrea family, 37
McCumber, Mr. James, 22, 32
McEachern family, 11
McKinnon, Luther, family, 20
McKoy family, 21
McLauchlin family, 9, 10, 15, 19
McLin Drug Store, 38
McMillan, W. Dougald, 36
McQueen, Mr. Knox, 16
McRary, William (church donation), 23
Meares House, 36

Moore, Duncan, 8
Morgan, Rufus (photographer), inside front cover, 24
Moss, Mary Bonner, 21
Mozella (enslaved spinner), 14
Murchinson Bank, 37
Murray, Eli (church donation), 23

N
Nancy (enslaved dairywoman), 28
Nash, Mrs. Maria (school teacher), 8
National Bank, 38
Nixon, Mr. Nicholas (supplied food to Bellamys), 14
North Carolina Society of Colonial Dames, 23, 24, 26

O
Old Ladies Home, 22

P
Parsley family, 4, 5, 9, 16
Pearce House, 37
Peoples & Atlantic Bank, 38
Phillips, Rev. Charles (Presbyterian), 23
Potter, Gilbert, House, 37

R
Railroads, IX, 5, 8, 20, 37
Rankin family, 16, 17
Ransom, Robert (Chief of Police), 25
Record (Negro newspaper), 8
Red Springs, 20
Richmond (enslaved shoemaker), 14
Riot of 1898, 8
Rothwell, Laura, 17, 21
Russel family, 11, 13, 17, 21

S
Sanders, Mr. John A. (brought food to Bellamys), 13
Sarah (enslaved cook), 6
Scuffletown, 16
Seaman's Bethel, 38
Session House, 37
Shoe Heel Depot, 20
Slaves, VII, IX, 6, 7, 12-15, 20, 28, 33
Smith family (Roomer), 18, 27
Smithville *see Southport*

Society of Colonial Dames
 see NC Society of Colonial Dames
South Carolina Female Institute
 see Barhamville School
Southern Building, 37
Southport, 26
Sprunt family, 24, 27, 38
Stallings, Miss Lina (companion), 18, 34, 40
Steinberg, Mr. (teacher), 21
Steward Hall (Floral College), 5, 12
Sherman, General William T. (Union), IX, 22, 34
Swann family, 9, 19

T
Taylor family, 13, 17, 30, 39
Tennant, E.S. family, 39
Tony (enslaved handyman), 7
Turpentine Plantation (owned by Dr. John D. Bellamy), 10, 15
Turrentine, Rev. M.C. (minister to slaves at Grovely), 6

U
Union Army, VIII, IX, X, XI, 4-7, 9, 11-16

V
Verner family, 18, 23, 30, 31

W
Waddell, A.M. (Mayor), 8, 25, 36
Walker House, 36
Watson, Major, 9-11
Williamson, Eliza Bellamy (niece), 24
Wilmington map, 46, 47
Wilmington, map of surrounding area, 48, 49
Wooster, Willie, 8
Wright House
 see Burgwin-Wright House
Wright, Silas (Mayor), 8

Y
Yankees *see Union Army*
Yellow fever epidemic, X, 4, 17, 30, 31, 36